THE COMPLETE BOOK OF
Football Instruction

THE COMPLETE BOOK OF
Football Instruction

TOM CAPOZZOLI

Contemporary Books, Inc.
Chicago

Library of Congress Cataloging in Publication Data

Capozzoli, Tom, 1927–
    The complete book of football instruction.

    Includes index.
    1. Football coaching.   2. Football—Training.
I. Title.
GV956.6.C37   1981   796.332'07   81-65175
ISBN 0-8092-5836-6   AACR2
ISBN 0-8092-5874-9 (pbk.)

Interior photos by George Rau and Tom Capozzoli

Published by Contemporary Books, Inc.
180 North Michigan Avenue, Chicago, Illinois 60601
Manufactured in the United States of America
Library of Congress Catalog Card Number: 81-65175
International Standard Book Number: 0-8092-5836-6 (cloth)
                                    0-8092-5874-9 (paper)

Published simultaneously in Canada by
Beaverbooks, Ltd.
150 Lesmill Road
Don Mills, Ontario M3B 2T5
Canada

"To Carole . . . for believing."

Contents

KEY TO DIAGRAM ABBREVIATIONS

B	back
C	center
E	end
G	guard
K	kicker
T	tackle
DB	defensive back
DE	defensive end
DL	defensive linemen
DT	defensive tackle
FB	fullback
FL	flanker
HB	halfback
LB	linebacker
LH	left halfback
LS	left safety
NG	nose guard
OG	offensive guard
OL	offensive linemen
OT	offensive tackle
QB	quarterback
RB	running back
RH	right halfback
SE	split end
TE	tight end
WB	wingback
WR	wide receiver
LCB	left cornerback
LOS	line of scrimmage

Introduction

Football is a game of skill and technique. There are hundreds of tasks to be performed, and each of them requires specific actions that must be done in certain ways to increase your chances of success. Football also requires physical strength, coordination, and timing; for the most part, these abilities can be developed or enhanced if you haven't come by them naturally. Finally, there's that special ingredient called courage, which players have in varying amounts and is so necessary on so many occasions.

If all of this makes football sound like an unpleasant sport to play, forget it. Football is a great game, filled with excitement and thrills. Boys who play it want to keep playing it, and when their participation ends they continue to pursue the sport as fans of local football teams, college teams, or professional teams. In fact, most of them become fanatics because they can't get enough of the atmosphere, the excitement, and the keen competition among the teams. The key word here is *competition* because it is the driving force behind the motivation that spurs players on to be successful. In order to be successful, you must learn the skills well, and you must be physically prepared to use those skills as well as your ability will allow. Herein lies the purpose of this book—to teach you how to perform the techniques of football and to explain the many factors that influence the outcome of the game.

This book is intended for young football players and their coaches who are anxious to learn more about the game. Football instructions fit into two basic categories: the things that players do as individuals, and the things they have to do with other players as a team. Both aspects are covered in considerable detail and will help the young player to understand what he has to do to be successful.

Football is learned through instruction and through execution. Instruction may be obtained by reading what has to be done; or by working under the direction of coaches, who show players what to do and how to do it. Execution is the actual performance of the techniques on the field. This book provides the young player with specific instructions about every position, enabling him to practice his execution and technique before and during each football season.

Coaches, too, will benefit from this book because it explores both the basic fundamentals and the finer points of this very complex sport. There are hundreds of topics covered that are vital to a successful football program. The instructions are specifically geared to the requirements of pre-high school and high school level teams and include offensive and defensive formations, the basic concepts of passing and rushing, special teams, and all the unique skills that players and teams must be trained for.

In addition, there are dozens of photographs and sketches which illustrate the techniques provided in the text. Once you have read this book, you will know a great deal more about the game and have a much better chance of succeeding as an effective football player or coach.

1 | What It Takes to Excel in Football

DESIRE TO IMPROVE YOUR SKILLS

Each of us was born with a different level of natural athletic ability. These abilities allow some of us to be successful in one sport, others in many sports. When boys start playing football they usually don't know whether their talent is average, below average, or above average. They begin with a desire to play and when they start to get more deeply involved they begin to discover exactly where they stand in terms of talent and ability. In my coaching career, I have known boys whose ability was way above average but who had little motivation to improve on it. Others, with little or no ability, have worked and worked to become good enough to participate. The main point here is that you must recognize that you will have to adjust your approach to the game based on the level of ability at which you begin. Everyone can im-

prove, and if you apply yourself as diligently as possible, you will get all you can from the game.

Unfortunately, many boys who are endowed with great natural ability fail to reach their full potential. This is often true of boys who began to be successful at an early age: they observe that they are better than most of the other boys and consequently decide that they don't have to keep trying to improve. It is far better to take a different approach. Namely, if you have enjoyed some degree of success and are enjoying the game because of it, think of how much more you will enjoy it if you improve in your ability. Also consider that you may be one of the few players who are good enough to go on to the next level of football as you grow older.

When boys start playing in youth leagues before they enter high school, they often assume that they will keep playing the game forever, or at least during junior and senior high school.

Pregame color and excitement as a college band and majorettes perform for 77,000 people in the stadium.

Unfortunately, this is not usually true. As you go up the ladder of football levels, the competition gets tougher because the players have had more years in which to improve their skills. It holds true then that, if you don't keep pace with them, you will soon become a fan because you will no longer be qualified as a player. Under normal circumstances the boys with greater ability can get by because the coaches can easily recognize their ability and will select them as members of their squads. It is sad, however, when boys of lesser ability, who have tried to improve their skills, have failed to impress the coaches and are cut from the squad.

Whether your ability is good or poor, you will never know what your competition will be when you go out for a team. Doesn't it make sense, then, that you should try to improve as much as you can at each level? This has two benefits: first, by striving as hard as you can to improve, you will enjoy the level of ball that you are currently playing; and second, you will be getting yourself ready for the sterner competition ahead of you at the next level up the ladder.

In summary, you must have a strong desire to improve your ability if you want to get the most *you* can get out of the game. If you have no natural desire to excel, you should try to develop one. This is easily done by simply reading the success stories of any of the outstanding players in the college or professional ranks. They couldn't have gotten where they are if they lacked a strong desire to succeed. This is true not only in all sports but also in all professions as well. Sometimes the desire results from friendly competition between brothers or among neighbors or classmates. You can see it in the way boys strive to outdo each other in simple one-on-one games. You may also see this competitive spirit when a father tells his son that he is better than his brother was or when a coach tells a young athlete that he had the fastest time in the forty-yard run. Look around and you will see the struggle to achieve and succeed everywhere, but most particularly in the sports world, where ability alone will not guarantee success unless it is coupled with dedication and a desire to continue to improve every day in every way.

DEDICATION AND LOYALTY TO YOUR TEAM

Other motivations are available to give you the desire to excel. When you become a member of a team you are given a position to play. That position is vital to the success of the team. All positions are vital to the success of a team. Your responsibility to the team and your teammates is to play that position as well as you can. Sometimes that isn't good enough, in which case the coach will often replace you with another player. This other player may not have as much ability as you have, but he may have a stronger desire to improve. When you are replaced by someone with more ability than you, you can usually shrug if off and say that you understand why the coach replaced you. But, when the other player has equal or less talent, you will understandably put yourself down for letting it happen. You may also feel embarrassed in front of your friends because your apparent failure is available for everyone to see. Therefore, when you find yourself in this kind of situation, don't wait until it is too late to react. Make up your mind that you are going to give it everything you have and hold up your end of the team by being the best player you can be. It is a sad chore for a coach to replace one player with another. Later we will discuss one of the most important decisions a coach must make—determining which boys should play and which boys should be substitutes. A team cannot survive without second- and third-string players, but all members would like to be on the first string because first-string players get more playing time in games. All the boys on the squad have to practice every week, but only a small percentage play in the games. And the real rewards of the sport are found mostly in the playing of the games. If you want to share in all that fun and excitement, you must work as hard as you can to impress your coach and get yourself as high up on his depth chart as you can.

Dedication to your team is also expressed in the way you conduct your life. In order to do your best for your team you have to be prepared mentally as well as physically. Most of this book will deal with the physical aspects of preparation, but it is important to note what some of the mental requirements are as well. For example, when you are on a school team your eligibility to play is based on having passing grades in all your subjects. Coaches are often upset by key players who have not done their school work well enough and have been ruled ineligible to play by the school's administration. It's a letdown for the members of a team when one of their key players is not allowed to play because of his grades. Your commitment to your school team must include the desire to do well in your studies. Otherwise, the team will not only be deprived of your services, but will also be depressed because they will know that their team is not as strong as it should be. Perhaps even more important is the fact that you will suffer from poor grades because you won't be as capable a student and, further, if you are talented enough to go on to college ball, your chances of getting a scholarship will be reduced by poor grades that appear on your transcript.

The other aspect of mental preparation involves knowing what your assignments are according to your position. Contrary to popular belief, football requires a great deal of intelligence to play well. Even at the early stages, the

Players of both teams gather around to dedicate themselves to a team victory.

game has become more complex than it ever was. Youth leagues have installed a wide variety of plays that require youngsters to study and learn many different assignments on different plays. They also learn to cope with a wide assortment of techniques, both offensively and defensively. You will also find young players playing both ways, which means they have to learn what to do in both situations. This situation is usually less common when you get to high school, though many small high schools still have most of their players playing both offense and defense.

It is not until you get to college that you begin to see one-way players. This reduces the amount of data they have to learn, but, at the same time, the complexity of the college game broadens year after year. Therefore, the one-way college players end up having to study and learn much more than the average two-way player in high school. It would be wise, then, to approach this game from a point of view that says you must be prepared to study thoroughly all the mental aspects of the game or you will be putting an extra burden of failure on yourself. When a blocking assignment, for example, is missed and a defensive player breaks through and throws the quarterback for a big loss, the coach will immediately ask who was responsible for the blown assignment. When he finds out that it was you, a black mark will be etched in his mind alongside your name for future reference. If you should also miss practice during the following week, the coach may think that you have let the team down too many times and you may be replaced by another player.

The conclusion to be reached is that your desire to succeed must include mental as well as physical preparation. Mentally, try to learn all there is to learn. This not only includes what your coaches teach you, but also what you can learn by watching games in person or on television. Watch the players who play your position and observe the things they do in various situations. All sports require the players to be able to react to adjust to certain conditions, but football uses more strategy than most and the strategy can only come from knowing what to do when your opponent does something to counter what

you are doing to him. This is probably the most significant part of the mental approach to the game: what you should do differently to give you the best chance of success with the guy across the line of scrimmage from you. The choices of what you should do will be provided to you by your coaches, but the ability to select which one to use at which time is usually based on your instant reaction to what you remember of what you were taught. You can see, therefore, that football is a game of brains versus brains as well as of bodies versus bodies.

COURAGE TO FACE PHYSICAL ORDEALS

Among other things, football is a game of courage. This word is used in many different ways, but to the football coach it usually means that you have to do what football requires of you *without fear*. The reason is that fear often causes a player to fail to do something as well as his ability will allow. If a boy has learned how to tackle, for example, but suddenly becomes afraid that the big fullback coming at him will cause him bodily injury and pain, he will probably shy away and miss the tackle. Or, if a quarterback is afraid that his pass will be intercepted and he will be criticized for it, he may throw badly and fail to complete it. It is for these reasons and many, many others that coaches try to train players to react automatically, *without fear*. They also try to repeat, over and over, frequently experienced situations so the player will do them by reflex action, often without even taking the time to think about what he is doing.

When a boy learns that in the great majority of times a tackle does not cause him physical pain, he will no longer think about the size and shape of the ball carrier; he will simply go in for the tackle. Likewise, when the quarterback sees that the coach understands that interceptions are part of the game, and the quarterback has taken all the necessary precautions, he will throw the ball as well as he can without fear of interception. This kind of fear is usually called anxiety and is not physical fear but mental fear. It can have the same kind of effect on the player, however, causing him to fail to do what his ability will normally allow him to do. Only through constant practice and through game experience will a player be able to condition himself to the point at which he can ignore these distractions and perform in direct relation to his training, ability, and poise.

Another kind of fear is related to a dislike for the extended physical activity so often required in a football program. These conditions usually occur during practice sessions. They most often involve the training, running, and reaction drills that a coach must put the team through in order to prepare them for the season and for each game on the schedule. Many of these will be covered in a later chapter. The point to be made here is that many players dislike the rigors of practice and many tend to abstain from giving their best on these occasions. This is probably the biggest problem a coach has to wrestle with because he knows that unless a team learns to practice well it will rarely become a good team.

The boys who want to become good players must resign themselves to the fact that they will have to put aside their fears and anxieties about the rigors of practice and recognize that it is all part of having a good team and becoming good players. It was mentioned earlier that frequent situations must be repeated often in practice if a player is to handle them automatically. It is here on the practice field that these repetitions must occur, and they must be done with the same effort, energy, and enthusiasm with which they will be done on Saturday afternoon in the stadium. If players try to hold something back in their practice execution, they will either use the same approach in a game or be forced to take a new approach for which they will not be fully prepared. The situation in which a player tackles a big fullback is a good example to illustrate this point. If a defensive safety makes a half-hearted tackle of a second-stringer in practice, he may have the same reflex reaction in a game and miss the all-important tackle of the fullback. The point is that full effort is required at all times. This means that when the coach tells you to run sprints up and down the field, you have to do it with the same energy and desire as if you were running for a touchdown or chasing an opposing halfback heading for your goal line. Put aside your fear of practice. Look at practice as an opportunity to develop your skills and abilities and as a chance to impress your coaches.

Coaches usually evaluate the abilities of players mainly through their practice performance. With this in mind, do you want your coach to think that you are running as fast as you can when you are putting out half-speed in the wind sprints? When a coach sees a slacker in practice, he often concludes that the player will slack off in a game, too. The process of determining which boys are better than others is a constant one that goes on from the first day of practice to the last one at the end of the season. You will never know when your coach is looking at you and you can't take the time to keep looking over your shoulder to see whether or not he is looking. Therefore, be smart and accept the fact that if you want to play instead of sit, and you want to be the best player you can be, you must be a good practice player.

NEED FOR A TRAINING PROGRAM

All players, regardless of age, ability, and experience, need a training program to develop or improve their skills or to develop their bodies or sharpen their conditioning to its finest edge. Once you begin your football career, and you have decided which position you will play, you must develop a training program that is suited to that position. For example, a weights program designed to build up the strength of an interior lineman is not recommended for a quarterback.

Each position has skills in common with some other positions but also has skill requirements unique to that position. As each position is reviewed in subsequent chapters, the skill requirements that pertain to each of them will be covered in much detail. You may be tempted to turn directly to the chapter that covers your position and pore over the information that applies to you, but it is recommended that you read all the chapters and their skill requirements because you may find other positions that your skills and physical capabilities match.

Going out for a football team at any age level is associated with certain key decisions. If you tell the coach that you would like to try out for a position of your choosing, it may cause a problem between you and the coach because many boys may be interested in the same position and your chances of making the team or of becoming a regular will be slim. On the other hand, if you determine that you have the potential to play more than one position, and you explain that to the coach, he will have a better opportunity to use you in one or more places on his depth chart, thereby increasing your chances of making the team at a variety of positions. So, if you are a relative newcomer to the game, review each position carefully to give yourself the best chance of success. And, if the coach should recommend that you try a totally different position, try to go along with him. After all, he has experience and a knowledge of the game behind him and he may be able to recognize a talent in you that you may not see. A coach often gets turned off when a boy refuses to agree to a position change because it appears that the boy is more interested in himself than he is in the team.

If you are an experienced player with a few years of playing behind you, your position is often already established. There are many instances, however, when a boy's position keeps changing right into college and sometimes even into the pro leagues. But, if you are heading into a season, you have every right to expect that the position you have been playing is the one you will probably play. With that in mind, your task is to develop a training program that will get you as ready as you can be for the season. When you review the chapter that applies to your position, try to identify the things on which you need the most improvement. Every player knows his strengths and weaknesses, probably better than anyone, including his coach. With all the high-level football on display on television, boys usually associate themselves with an outstanding player on a higher-level team who plays the same position. When you watch these really good players, you can see them do outstanding things, many of which you would like to be able to do. Make a vow to

yourself that you will honestly identify areas in which you need improvement and set yourself to the task of improving your skills in those areas.

Training is often a tiring task. It requires much repetition and can become boring if it is not done in the right way. For example, if you are trying to increase your speed by running a series of wind sprints, doing it alone makes it difficult to find new incentives. But if a group of boys try to race each other in the sprints, they will find themselves enjoying it more and getting much more out of it. Try not to let your training become a simple routine; find a way to spice it up as much as you can.

DRIVE TO ACHIEVE GOALS

The objectives of a training program are to achieve goals for yourself. In this case, the goals are the development of your skills. When you find yourself at the start of a new season, take the time to list the goals you want to accomplish during the year. As mentioned above, you may want to increase your speed. Refer to what your last speed timing was, perhaps during the previous year's season, and set a target for improvement of that speed for this year. Don't make the mistake of setting too tough a target for yourself because if you fail to achieve it you may become discouraged. It is far better to lower your sights a little and, once you've made it, set another goal for yourself. This will make you much more success-oriented, which is a good quality for an athlete to develop.

Try to be generous with the goals you establish. This means that they should be set in many different areas that relate to your body skills and to the tasks that you will be required to perform at your position. For example, there are weight and strength levels established for those positions that require specific degrees of strength. You can determine how much weight you should be able to lift for your height and weight. There are also speed requirements set for positions such as wide receivers and running backs. There are specific techniques that have to be learned, such as running pass routes for a receiver. And endurance standards are set for distance running that will help you develop the stamina and staying power that football demands of its players as the game wears on into the last period. If you are intent on giving it your best shot, you must become goal-oriented and maintain your high standards both at the beginning of the season and throughout the season.

REWARDS FOR OUTSTANDING PERFORMANCE

There are many things we do in life that bring us little or no reward for a job well done. Football is not one of those things. Many rewards are available to you if you are willing to pay the price for them. The particular price you will have to pay depends on the amount of effort you will have to devote to become capable of outstanding performances. All the things that have been covered in this chapter point in practically the same direction—how to succeed as a player in the demanding game of football. Although it is a team-oriented sport, football demands that its players be prepared to perform their individual tasks in order to be successful.

Following the same logic, the rewards are both team rewards and individual ones. It is far more satisfying for a player who performs well to have his team win than lose. But, even if your team loses, if you did your very best you can hold your head high with that knowledge. In other words, even though no one enjoys losing, there is a certain satisfaction in knowing that you held up your end. It is the realization that the personal targets you strived for have made it possible for you to give a good account of yourself. It amounts to an inner sense of accomplishment that all players try to achieve every time they set foot on a field.

When you look back on what you did during a game, you often find things that did not turn out the way you wanted them to. These are the things that you should try to eliminate the next time you play—your new goals. It is a sad young man who can readily identify a mistake that he made that may have caused the team to lose the game. This should become an even stronger incentive for improvement that will prevent it from happening again.

Without doubt, the biggest satisfaction to be had from football is the combination of an effective individual effort and a solid team effort that has resulted in not only a victory but a championship as well. There is something magical about the feeling that overcomes everyone because the team members know how much effort—often blood and sweat—went into making it happen. This is the big goal that everyone associated with football usually dreams of and, when it is met, you realize that every ounce of energy, dedication, and effort that you put into getting ready for the season was worth it.

LOVE FOR THE GAME

It takes more than winning championships to make players put out 1000 percent week after week, season after season. When you have been playing the game for a while, you begin to realize that you have developed a love for the game that most football players feel is very unique to the sport. To be honest, many of the same satisfactions can be had while playing other sports. And there are athletes who believe that football players exaggerate the qualities of football in their attempts to set it apart from and

The two teams await the start of the game to reap the rewards of hard work and practice.

above other sports. But, when other boys who have played sports besides football are consulted on this subject they most often say that football is special. They may be hard pressed to explain why they feel that way, but if you press them on it you may hear something like the following:

"When you play a game that requires the finesse of a quarterback and a wide receiver—and the strength and rigors of a down lineman—and you couple them with the pain and dirt and sweat of a hard fought game, you begin to realize that this game welds together all the people who play it on any kind of team, whether it be youth football or the Super Bowl in January." Football teammates are teammates for life and their memories will never fade into obscurity. These are only some of the reasons players love the game. There are many, many more, and we'll find them as we proceed through the book.

2 | Offensive Philosophy and Strategy

THE MULTIPLE OFFENSE PHILOSOPHY

When coaches decide to use a variety of offensive formations, they commit themselves to a great deal of additional work to give their teams a much greater chance of success. This is true because football has become a much more complex game of strategy than ever before. Unless an assortment of techniques are available with which you can score, you may be hard pressed to win football games. Defenses are also becoming more sophisticated and difficult to penetrate, so a wise coach will try to provide his team with different weapons for scoring.

An opposing view is supported by some coaches, who believe that if you learn one offense very well, you don't have to bother with a multiple offense system and you will probably avoid putting as much pressure on your players to learn. They also support making minor adjustments to their single-offense system to find different ways to beat a tough defense. However, this attitude seems to be fading in favor of multiple-offense football. For one thing, coaches of football below the college level have found, perhaps to their surprise, that youngsters who make the commitment to play football want to learn as much as possible that will give them a better opportunity to win. And they want to do things in the same fashion as they see on TV in the college and professional ranks, which is predominantly multiple-offense football. There are only a few college coaches who don't use this system; and all the professional teams use it, many because they had to to remain competitive.

Now that we've discussed its relative merits, let's take a look at what multiple-offense football really means. Some formations are better suited for a running offense which places greater

MULTIPLE OFFENSIVE FORMATIONS
PASSING ORIENTED

PRO-SET LEFT

PRO-SET RIGHT

WIDE SLOT LEFT

WIDE SLOT RIGHT

TWIN RIGHT–SLOT LEFT

TWIN LEFT–SLOT RIGHT

A wide-out pro set offensive formation provides an excellent passing offense.

emphasis on strong running backs powering the ball; other offensive sets are more useful to support a strong passing game. This chapter is intended to provide young players with a deeper knowledge of offensive formations and the strategy involved in their use.

A coach will usually use the offense that best suits his personnel. If he has good passing talent along with good receiving skills, he will be far more successful if he uses the spread or wide-out formations, such as some of those in the diagrams on page 10.

These formations are intended to attack the entire width of the field and to put pressure on every defender to do his job without making mistakes. Pass-oriented, they also tend to open up the running game because the defenders have to spread out in order to provide adequate defensive strength. If the defense forgets to cover twin receivers to one side, then one of them is likely to be open to receive a pass. In lower levels of football, where mistakes like this are more apt to happen, an attentive coach and/or quarterback can quickly exploit such oversights and make substantial gains. A careless defense can make many other mistakes that a wide-open offense can take advantage of. Many of these will be

covered later in the text as we review the responsibilities of the various positions. When a coach sees that the team's best talent is in the rushing area, and he doesn't have any players with real passing skills, he should lean toward the power

A twins left formation gives two wide receivers many pass patterns to exploit the defense.

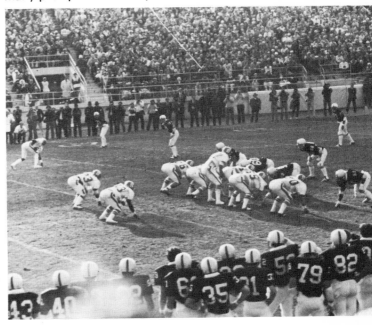

RUNNING FORMATIONS

POWER I

WISHBONE

WING LEFT

WING RIGHT

I-SLOT LEFT

I-SLOT RIGHT

The wing right formation with a split end gives the offense both running and passing capabilities.

running type of offensive formations such as those sketched in the diagrams on page 12.

These formations all tend to support a strong blocking approach to the game by putting players in position to perform a variety of blocks on a variety of defensive personnel. The basic idea is to prevent the defense from knowing how you are going to attack them by using formations that can attack many different areas along the line of scrimmage. Their use does not mean that the forward pass is put away in mothballs. On the contrary, the pass becomes the unexpected weapon that many coaches would prefer it to be, rather than the wide-open sets when everyone knows that you are going to throw.

A team's philosophy of offense should depend, therefore, on what its talents are and what it can do best. As a player, you have to make a decision as to where your talents best fit into the team's offense and where the coach thinks your skills can help the team the most. This can sometimes be a very sensitive point between coach and player, but it has to be worked out amicably to help foster the right attitudes on the team.

The two tight end formation (with a flanker) allows for power running with some passing potential.

HOW TO CONFUSE THE DEFENSES

There are many views on how to run an offense successfully. They are as plentiful as there are different coaches. There is one area of agreement, however, and that is to find as many ways as possible to confuse the defense. Many of the techniques used can be used by any of the above formations, but others have a much better chance of success with one particular formation or another. For example, one of the most frequently used plays to cross up a defense is the draw play. It is used when the defense expects you to throw a pass and you surprise them by handing off to a running back instead. The *pro right draw* is one of my favorite draw plays, and it has given the teams I coached many long gains in many crucial spots in tough games (see diagram). The strategy is based on the fact that because the wide-out offense gives the team a better opportunity to throw the ball more successfully, the defense is going to expect the offense to pass a great deal. You then proceed to do just that, and after showing the defensive linemen that if they don't get to the quarterback the offense is going to beat their secondary, the linemen start coming at you full tilt. This is the right time to use the draw play against them. It is the unexpected and, when it results in a wide-open hole in their front and a long gain, they are forced to become more cautious and slow

down their rush. Once this happens, your passing game gets the benefit of more time for the quarterback to pick out an open receiver. And, as you proceed to beat their secondary again, the linemen start to rush wildly again; then it is time for the draw play to do its thing again. And it goes on and on and on.

There is one thing that must not be overlooked, however, and that is that you must correctly perform each of the above or your plan goes down the drain. Unless you throw and catch the ball well, the defensive linemen will not respect your passing game and will not have to rush the passer without caution. Your draw play will then fail more often than it succeeds. Once again, it is obvious that skill and technique are paramount to success.

A wide assortment of misdirection plays can be blended successfully into many different offensive sets. A few of the most commonly used are known as *counter plays, reverses, crossbucks,* and *bootlegs.* Let's look at each of them to see what they offer the offense and what players should understand about their usefulness and strategy.

The *counter play* is one in which the ball starts going in one direction but ends up going in another, or counter, direction. Many teams use a version of the I formation. One of its most frequently used plays is a *counter slant* (see diagram). In this play, the offense looks like it is using a standard blast play in which the half-

PRO-RIGHT DRAW

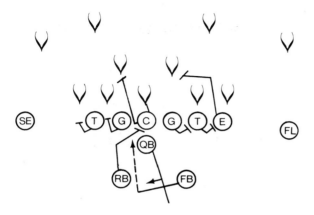

I-SLOT LEFT-COUNTER

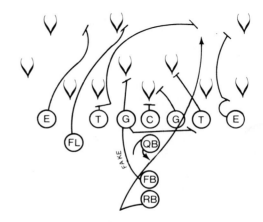

back follows the fullback into the left guard/left tackle hole area; but, as soon as the halfback gets the ball, he slants away from the left side of the line in order to hit the hole opened for him on the right side of the line. The confusion results when the linebackers, moving to stop the blast, find themselves out of position to stop the *counter*. When they are out of position they are easier to block by the offensive linemen, who have gained an advantage through the deception in the offensive backfield.

The quarterback's reverse pivot also disguises whether he has the ball or has handed off. This will keep the secondary honest because there are other play action passes in which the quarterback fakes to the halfback and throws a quick pass. Take note of the left guard, who pulls out and traps the off-side tackle to make the hole really open up. Once again, the fake into the left side makes the off-side tackle feel safe; but he soon finds that he is trapped and has failed to cover his part of the defensive line. When you can fool the defense, you have gained an advantage.

A *reverse* is another way to mislead the defense. This play becomes more inviting when a defensive team is occupied by pursuing your outside running game. Let's assume that we are running end sweeps and gaining a lot of yardage. The defense realizes that it is one of our strong weapons against them and that they are going to have to react quickly in order to keep us from beating them with it. Their answer is to counter our speed with their speed, and they start to pursue wildly as we apparently run

outside of them again (see diagram). When the quarterback turns and pitches to the halfback, and the guards pull to lead the ball carrier around end, the defensive front and the linebackers take an angle of pursuit to prevent the ball carrier from turning the corner. It is at this moment that the ball is handed off to the fleet flanker, who has discreetly moved into position to receive the handoff and is prepared to fly around the other end with a key block required on the defensive right end. All other offensive players must try to prevent penetration by the defense or the play will end up losing yardage. This is not a play that is recommended for use more than once or twice a game, nor is it wise to use it near the opponent's goal line because their attention is usually focused more strongly on that part of the field. In addition, end sweeps are usually not used in attacking the goal line because any kind of penetration can result in a big loss.

Crossbucks were probably the first misdirection plays used in the early days of football, but they still have usefulness in certain offensive sets. The *wishbone* formation, so popular in the early 1970s, is starting to fade from use in many parts of the United States. However, many coaches believe it is the best rushing-oriented offense that ever existed and continue to use it. The *crossbuck* is one of the preferred plays for the *wishbone* formation, and it is executed in many ways. One of them is illustrated in the diagram. The *wishbone* can use a few two-on-one blocking situations anywhere on the line of scrimmage. For this reason, the linebackers must

PRO RIGHT–REVERSE LEFT

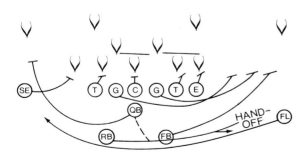

WISHBONE CROSSBUCK

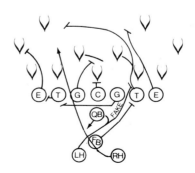

react quickly to fill the holes that these blocks create. In addition, linemen away from the ball have to try to slide along the line of scrimmage to help out in the attacking area. It is for these reasons that a misdirection play like the *cross-buck* is as successful as it is.

When the fullback apparently leads the left halfback into the right guard/tackle hole, the defense immediately reacts. Therefore, when the right guard pulls quickly behind the center and traps the right defensive tackle, the hole is opened and the linebacker is not there to fill the hole. Depending on the success of the other blocks, the play may gain a lot of yardage. More importantly, when used on many occasions it forces the defense to "stay at home," an expression that means the linebacker and the off-side linemen should not try to rush to the apparent attack area until they are sure that it is not a *counter play* that will come at their area. This helps the offense because it will cut down on the number of people they have to block at the attack area and increases their chances of success, which, after all, is one of the benefits that *counter plays* are intended to give an offense.

The *bootleg* is another play that can't be used very often because it tends to make the defense too conscious of it. Nonetheless, it is an important part of the arsenal of misdirection plays.

PRO-LEFT–BOOTLEG RIGHT

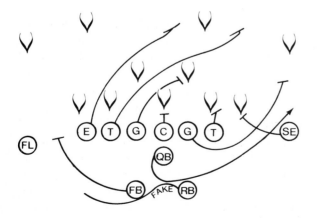

One of my favorites is illustrated in the diagram. The main thrust in this play is deception. Everyone on the team must make the play look like it is a sweep around the left end, particularly the would-be ball carrier, the halfback. The quarterback must practice his technique often to make sure that he has it down to a science. If he fails to perform well, the confusion that is being sought will not occur and the play will lose yardage.

There are a few situations that give this play a better chance of success. If a defensive end is pursuing a run around the other end, he is failing to fulfill his responsibility to protect his end against a *counter play*. It is the same mistake that will usually make a *reverse* go well. When opposite-side defensive linemen fail to penetrate and begin to slide down the line of scrimmage, this also makes this and other misdirection plays succeed.

However, to make sure that the play has the best chance of success, the pulling of a guard to block the back-side end tends to guarantee that the quarterback will get around the corner, where he will be on his own against the people in the secondary. Although this play is seen more often in lower levels, where ends tend to make more mistakes in their defensive assignments, it is not unusual to see it in college and also in professional ranks because it truly is a surprise play that requires very little effort. In fact, on some occasions quarterbacks in the National Football League (NFL) have failed to tell their teammates that they were going to use the play and have simply failed to hand off to the halfback on a sweep, going the other way all by themselves.

The Mixture of Running and Passing

Regardless of which offensive sets are used, most coaches believe that it is necessary to mix rushing and throwing in significant amounts in order to vary their offensive strategy. We have illustrated how some formations make running easier to accomplish, while others enhanced the passing game. In either case, it is not wise to become oriented too far in one way or the other. However, arriving at the right mix is always a matter of concern and it should be arrived at with logic and good pregame planning.

If the team you are playing has weaknesses, your game plan should be geared to attack those weaknesses. Many times the weaknesses you see are in an area in which you are also weak. For example, if you run the ball very well and don't feature the passing game in your basic offense, then a team that has a weak pass defense will not be as significant to you as it would be to a passing-oriented team. However, that shouldn't stop you from trying to exploit their weaknesses. It simply means that during the week before the game you will have to stress more passing in your preparation to be at the top of your passing game. The other team knows you rush well and are going to overprepare to stop your strong running game, and are probably going to be unconcerned with your passing attack. When you throw passes against them—and you should throw as many as you have to—you will definitely have an advantage. The unexpected is always a benefit in your offense, especially when you do it well.

Many pass-minded teams tend to go overboard in their game planning strategy and end up throwing the ball too many times. The defensive approach against a passing offense is either to rush the passer so he has no time to throw or to put more people in the secondary to protect against the receivers running their pass routes. In either case, the defenses at the line of scrimmage tend to become weakened and susceptible to attack. Therefore, many coaches are becoming more and more pass-oriented, because it keeps the defense from loading up at the line and forces them to put more people in the secondary. In the process, passing teams have had to put more running into their offense to exploit this weakened area.

After a game plan has been devised in light of the opponent's strengths and weaknesses, adjustments and decisions must also be made during the game. When your opponent becomes aware of your strategy, he is likely to change in the course of the game and you have to be aware of what he is doing and when. In this regard, players have to contribute to the information getting to the coach and quarterback to make

them aware of what is going on in each area of the contest. For example, an offensive guard may see that the linebacker opposite him is retreating into the secondary on the snap of the ball to help in the pass protection. This knowledge, passed on to the quarterback, may lead to a running play through that area that results in a long gain that otherwise would not have been possible.

A good direction to all players is to let your coach know anything that your opponents are doing with any kind of regularity or in any pattern. The best scouting report cannot give information that is as reliable or as complete as you can get from your own team during a game. If this communication link is not divulging all the vital information that is available, an important aid to success is lacking. In addition to the players, the people who spot for the coach must also impart solid information based on what they see from the press box, the top of the stadium, or wherever they are placed to observe the defense's strategy. There are just so many things that can be adjusted during the course of a game and they must not be wasted on suggestions based on marginal information. Therefore, when the offensive unit comes off the field, the coach must gather as much data as possible to find out what went wrong and what must be done to do it in a better way.

BASIC CONCEPTS OF OFFENSE

The most basic concept behind a successful offense involves determining what you do best and finding as many ways as possible to do it. It goes without saying that players must find various ways in which to do their part in this approach to success. The coach will clearly spell out your role; then it is up to you to carry it out the best way you can. For example, let's say that your coach believes in using only a few plays and wants to practice them over and over until they can't be done any better. Your role would be to understand exactly what you are to do and then to execute that. On the other hand, if your coach gives you fifty different plays to learn, you had better study them well and try to guarantee a mistake-free performance at game time.

You have been given both extremes. These, as well as other less extreme cases, make up the basic concepts of offense. The *wishbone* offense tends to keep things simple with often repeated, very basic plays. A multiple-offense coach, on the other hand, will probably use many more plays in his offense. In high school or lower levels a player doesn't have much control over what he will encounter; but if you are going to play ball in college, you have an opportunity to choose which system you would prefer to use. There have been many capable passing quarterbacks who never had an opportunity to show what they could do because they played for a *wishbone* coach who hardly ever wanted them to throw the ball. There have also been many outstanding running backs who spent most of their time blocking for pass plays for a coach who liked to throw instead of run.

However, coaches are getting better every year because they are able to see the advances being made by other coaches at the college and professional levels. High schools are now playing a game that is just as wide open as the NFL game—and enjoying it just as much. The trend appears to be moving away from the "three yards and a cloud of dust" philosophy that many older coaches have used. And as more players come out of college, where they have played under multiple offenses, they will use those offenses in their coaching careers, and the players will find that football can be a very exciting and demanding game.

Selecting Offensive Personnel

Whatever your coach decides to do offensively, he will need to make good decisions regarding which players play which positions. In fact, these are probably the most important decisions he will make. You, as a player, must try to fit into his plans and try to make them match your plans, if possible. We will try to highlight what the coach will be looking for; you should try to see where you feel you would fit in best.

Coaches break down their initial search into two categories. They look for what are known as the *skilled positions*—quarterbacks, running backs, receivers, passers, and kickers. They also

look for the *strength positions*—interior linemen, both offensive and defensive, and the secondary people, including linebackers and defensive backs.

The skill people are put through a variety of throwing and catching drills through which running ability and speed are evaluated. Coordination will also be sought because it is a vital talent for all athletes to have and football is no exception. If a player can throw well, has good coordination, and is not too tall or too short, too thin or too heavy, he will be considered for the quarterback position. The boys who catch well will be divided into two categories: the slender, faster ones will become wide receivers, and the stronger, slower ones will become tight ends.

When speed running is measured by a stopwatch, the bulkier fast boys will become running back or linebacker candidates because both positions require strength and quickness. Many of the slender and fast receiver-types will also be diverted off to the defensive corps to play in the defensive secondary, where strong tackling ability is a must. The selection of centers, guards, and tackles basically comes from the same pool of talent. Players have to be big, rugged, tough, and able to withstand the rigors of physical activity over the course of a long game. Among these players, the guards will tend to be the shorter boys and the tackles the larger ones, with centers coming out of the tackle group. And when the actual tackling practices begin, the coach will choose the best defensive people from those who show a greater ability to be tough and to bring people down. The offensive interior linemen will be those who display greater blocking skill to go along with their quickness in getting off with the ball.

If your talent lies in your ability to kick the ball, you will have ample opportunity to display it when the coach asks for candidates for those important tasks or when he manages to see you during your many practice sessions.

All of the above will be discussed for each individual position in later chapters. This basic overview was intended to categorize briefly the basics that coaches and players encounter at the start of each season, when the important position/player decisions are made.

OFFENSIVE SKILLS TRAINING

This is another category of interest that will be covered in subsequent chapters, position by position. It is important for all players to realize that making the most progress is in their own hands and is accomplished through their own initiative and dedication. When you have determined what position you will most likely play, you must make a full-time effort to improve on your natural ability.

Probably the most important goal in offensive training for all football players is to improve their speed. How a player goes about improving his speed is one of the most frequently discussed aspects of the game. A track coach once said that running is a matter of picking up your legs and stretching them forward, and the boys who can do it more quickly will be the faster ones. It seems logical, then, that if you have strong thigh muscles, which are the primary muscles used to raise and lower your legs, you will be able to run faster than you would if your thigh muscles were not as well developed. Therefore, any exercising and/or leg strengthening you can do will probably increase your speed. In addition, speed is also increased through coordinated body control. The movement of your arms as you pump them while running has a direct bearing on the synchronized movement of your legs. You will never see a sprint man on a track team who has not mastered the harmony between his arms and legs. A starting stance is another important requirement for speed. Various positions require different stances, which will be covered in the chapters on individual positions. When you put them all together and you run often enough to develop them and your stamina, you will have reached the limits of your ability for your age. As you grow older and

your body develops, your ability to run faster will also improve if you continue to work on all the aspects mentioned above.

Other aspects of offensive skills also require consistent and constant practice. A passer has to throw often in order to develop the full strength of his arm and upper body. But he must also execute the passes in the same fashion as if he were throwing to a receiver in a game in order to develop the accuracy of his throwing ability. Therefore, it is strongly recommended that quarterbacks and receivers try to find time to do their practice together because one is dependent on the other. It is also good for their timing because it takes time for them to gear their teamwork. If a receiver is very fast, the quarterback will have to lead him farther downfield in order to ensure that the ball comes down to hit the receiver in full stride. Some quarterbacks can throw farther than others and the range of effectiveness can often be determined in this kind of one-on-one practice session.

The strength positions on the offensive front can also practice with each other to develop their blocking skills. They can take turns being the defensive tackle and give each other as many problems as they can to sharpen their abilities. Helmets and shoulder pads are all that is required for these one-on-one drills.

Whatever your position, there are ways you can improve your offensive skills. It will usually require you to do some specific planning to schedule a group of players at a given time on a certain day, but it will be worth your while when the day comes for the coach to select the players he believes are ready to take the field for your team. First-string players are those who have done the most to earn that honor and are usually the ones who have worked to do as much as they could have with their skills and abilities.

3 | The Making of a Quarterback

How to Choose a Quarterback

When a coach begins his search for talent he usually begins with the skilled positions. Perhaps the most difficult position to fill is that of the quarterback. It is so difficult because there are many talents that an athlete must possess in order to perform all the duties that the quarterback role requires. This position, more than any other, requires superb coordination, quick reflexes, gracefulness, and intelligence, to mention just a few of the qualities a coach must look for in a player. The coach will probably begin by trying to determine which boys can throw the ball best. This can be accomplished by simply having the candidates have a catch with each other.

Passing requires full body control and rhythm, which is another way of identifying the coordination of all body actions that are necessary to be a good passer. In general, there is a body type that most frequently is blessed with coordination. In high school and earlier, boys who have grown very tall at an early age fail to develop their coordination at the same pace. Similarly, boys who are heavier than their frames can handle also have difficulty with full control of their bodies.

An experienced coach also realizes that boys who are not well developed muscularly often cannot withstand the physical strain that frequently befalls a quarterback, so they tend to steer away from slightly built young athletes. Boys that are slow of foot are not able to react and move quickly enough to handle all the quarterback assignments, and boys who are too short to cope with the rigors of the position may also not be the best candidates.

THE PHYSICAL REQUIREMENTS

After making general observations of the body types that often are lacking in one way or another, the coach tries to find boys who have the qualities that most often are found in outstanding quarterbacks. Keep in mind that this is a general approach to the selection of a quarterback and may often be subject to exceptions to the rule. For instance, exceptional young men have played the position with skill and achieved outstanding results without having all the ideal physical traits. In the final analysis, a coach will use the best talent he can find on his squad. Our main thrust here is to begin the talent hunt with the body types that are most conducive to the execution of the quarterback role.

A coach should begin by looking for average height and strong but trim body weight. Probably the second most important traits are quickness and speed. The speed aspect can be measured by having the boys sprint against a stopwatch over a forty-yard course. This distance is the standard that almost all football teams use to identify the real speed of a player because it is more representative of the distance a player has to run in many game situations. In high school circles, a time of 5.0 seconds or less should be adequate for the quarterback position. If a boy is faster than that, the coach may want to consider him for a wide receiver or running back position, should some other boy be selected for the quarterback role. Speeds of 4.6 to 4.9 are rather rare in high school, particularly the lower ranges. Quickness can be assessed in many different ways, usually through reaction drills. One of the favorites is the drill in which the boys are asked to run between pylons or old tires in a zigzag pattern (see diagram).

The technique used here is to have each boy carry a football as he runs, moving it from one arm to the other as he passes each pylon, always holding the ball in the arm away from the obstacle. The other arm should be thrust at the pylon (dummies may be used instead) as though a straight arm were being used to ward off a would-be tackler. The boy's footwork must be as quick as possible, with short, controlled steps taken in order to maintain body balance and to avoid tripping as each tight circle is run around the obstacle. When the last pylon is passed, the boy must then prepare to hand off the ball to another boy, who is waiting to run his route in the opposite direction.

By observing all these coordinated activities, a coach can soon determine which boys handle them best. Many other drills, discussed later, may be used for the search for quickness. Timing, agility, and rhythm can be developed as the normal training of a quarterback occurs, but you should try to develop the coordination and quickness that are so essential to the quarterback.

THE PERSONALITY REQUIREMENTS

Many young players find it difficult to understand why there are personality requirements for various football positions. By personality we mean the characteristics that a boy possesses in his normal lifestyle as he mingles with his teammates and other people with whom he comes in contact. If a young player is well liked by his peers, he is likely to become a leader of his group. This is probably the most important quality that a coach looks for, because a quarterback is looked up to by a team. He must take

charge of a tough situation during a game when things are going badly, and it is necessary to rally the team to turn things around.

In this connection, a quarterback should also be a tough-minded individual who will not crack when the going gets rough. He has to snap back from a bad experience and show that he is not going to give up because of it. There are times when he may have to take one of the players to task for something done improperly. If he is not respected, the players may not accept his criticism favorably, which often leads to team unrest.

Naturally, a quarterback should also be admired by people around the school, not necessarily just those on the team. His overall behavior as a student and as a friendly person to schoolmates will come into view as a coach tries to determine who his quarterback should be. Boys who prefer to keep to themselves and not mingle readily with others will not give everyone an opportunity to know what they are like. This may lead to certain doubts in the minds of the coach and the members of the team as to what kind of a leader this person will be. And, without doubt, a boy who is a doer, someone who has developed a reputation for getting things done, will be looked on favorably because

there are so many things that must be done by a quarterback to ensure the smooth functioning of the team.

It also must be understood that all kinds of personalities go into the makeup of a team. There have been some outstanding players who hardly ever said a word to anyone, but when the game started they were in the thick of it, making as big a contribution as anyone. However, quarterbacks should be "holler" guys who can light the fires of their teammates and get them to do the things necessary for success.

BALL HANDLING TECHNIQUES—FROM THE CENTER TO THE QUARTERBACK

The quarterback handles the ball on every play except, in some instances, when kicking action occurs. The destiny of the team may rest on his ability to handle the ball well and to perform all the related functions with a minimum of errors. Usually, errors lead to fumbles, which lead to defeat more often than any other errors made on the field. In order to make ball handling the smooth action it must become, the coach will insist on many drills between quarterbacks and the ball carriers on the team. On

The quarterback takes his stance behind the center with feet spread, knees flexed, and hands ready for the ball.

each drill, he will direct the movement of the quarterback from the snap of the ball from the center to the actual handoff of the ball to the carrier.

The first technique to be learned is the transfer of the ball from the center to the quarterback. Some coaches instruct their quarterbacks to place the left hand up under the center's butt, while others prefer the right hand to be on top. Whichever is used, the basic requirement is to place the back of the hand firmly against the buttocks, with the opposite hand's heel almost touching the heel of the top hand. Both hands should be just below the curvature in a relaxed position to accept the thrust of the ball as it is brought up by the center. As soon as the ball hits the top hand, the bottom hand must quickly clamp on it to prevent it from squirting away.

The center should grasp the ball in such a way as to allow the laces to come up in the quarterback's throwing hand. This can be done by experimenting with the rotation of the ball as it is brought up from the ground to the quarterback's hands. The center should always instruct the referee as to how he would like to have the ball placed at the end of each play to avoid causing him to rotate it every time he comes out of the huddle. Officials are very cooperative because they know the importance of the exchange of the ball between the center and the quarterback.

The distance the quarterback stands behind the center is also important to the exchange. The quarterback's feet should be as wide apart as his shoulder width and they should be placed about six inches behind the center's feet. Knees should be flexed in a slight semicrouch position, which will allow the quarterback to turn in either direction after he has received the ball. Shoulders should be facing straight ahead, head turning slightly left and right to observe any movement in the defensive alignment, and fingers spread wide when the ball is snapped on the appropriate sound. The quarterback then must begin his footwork to get him into an area where he will exchange the football with a running back.

QUARTERBACK MOVEMENTS AWAY FROM THE CENTER

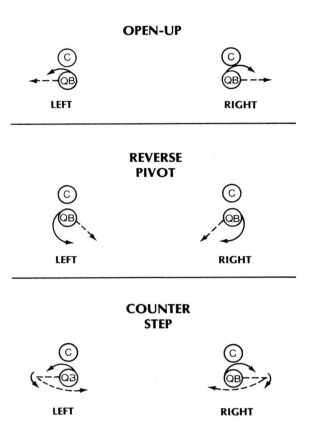

OPEN-UP

LEFT   RIGHT

REVERSE PIVOT

LEFT   RIGHT

COUNTER STEP

LEFT   RIGHT

FOOTWORK CONTROL—GETTING TO THE QUARTERBACK–RUNNING BACK HANDOFF

There are a variety of ways that the quarterback may move away from the center after receiving the snap (see diagram).

On the open-up step, he must push off his away leg and take the first step with his other foot while he is turning it and his body in that direction. The turning motion will be aided by the flexed-knees position of his original stance behind the center because his knees will not be locked in place. As he steps, the legs straighten out (unflex) and accelerate the body quickly away from the center. The quarterback must now begin to look for the running back and start to move toward the intersect point where the handoff will occur.

The quarterback takes an open-up step to the left and reaches out to hand the ball to the fast-starting running back.

The quarterback moves around the fullback (45) with the ball pulled in, heading for the handoff to the running back (43).

Ideally, the players will move in synchronization with each other as they seek to get as close as possible for the handoff without bumping into each other. The shorter the distance, the less likely a fumble will be. The running back must raise his arm that is closest to the quarterback while keeping the other arm tucked into his midsection to assist in the capturing of the ball when it is put firmly into his control. The running back must try to receive it with both of his hands grasping the ball and yet must allow the quarterback to press it into his hands without touching the quarterback's hands or arms. Any jostling in the exchange usually results in the ball being jarred loose, causing a fumble. After the ball is handed off, the quarterback must continue moving quickly away from the area, disguising the fact that he has given the ball away. On the reverse pivot movement away from the center, the quarterback again pushes off the foot that is not taking the first step as he turns 90 degrees and places the other foot in the direction of the running back. The quarterback must keep his body low to make him less visible to the defense and to help keep his body balance as he spins and heads into the backfield to the handoff point. The handoff uses the same technique described earlier, and the quarterback continues his deceptive moves away from the running back.

The counter-step technique begins in the same manner as the open-up step, since it brings the quarterback to the intersect point with the running back faking into the line. After taking the second step, which allows him to get close enough to perform the fake handoff, the quarterback must now turn 180 degrees, push off his far foot, and start moving in the opposite direction. This step is used often in the *wishbone* and *veer* offenses, in which the quarterback option plays are frequently used to put pressure on the defensive units.

MASTERING DECEPTION

On every occasion that a quarterback hands off to a running back, there is an opportunity for deception, the art of confusing the defense. When a coach takes the time to stress this skill, and the quarterback works at perfecting it, the offense benefits from the stress it puts on a defense. It is a series of techniques that must be practiced constantly in order to be done well. When done often, the actions become reflex actions.

Particularly in a pass-oriented offense, the location of the ball in the offensive backfield is vital to the defensive reaction of the opponent. For example, if a fake to a running back going into the line confuses a linebacker and makes him come up to make the tackle, he will not be in position to cover the tight end turning over the short middle for a quick pass (see diagram).

PRO-RIGHT QUICK PASS

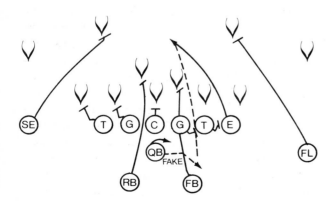

The running back comes forward to allow the quarterback to press the ball into his midsection on the handoff.

In many situations a misleading fake between the quarterback and a running back will gain an advantage. One of the most costly to the defense is when a safety rushes up toward the line of scrimmage to make a tackle on a sweep, only to find that the quarterback never handed the ball off to the running back, and the quarterback comes up, throwing a deep pass pattern to a crossing wide receiver deep in the safety's zone, and a touchdown is scored.

The best technique for deception is for you, as quarterback, to make the handoffs difficult to see by staying low and getting as close to the running back as you can, and by faking possession of the ball after you have handed it off. This is done best by either keeping your back to the defense as you run away from the line of scrimmage or making it look like you are holding the ball on your hip closest to your goal line as you run toward the sideline. The longer you continue the fake, the greater opportunity you have to fool someone on the defense. Even if you confuse only a few of them, you are likely to keep them away from the ball carrier.

Another common fake is used on a draw play in which the quarterback drops back and makes

The quarterback fakes possession of the ball by keeping his arms and hands in as he keeps his back to the defense.

everyone think he is going to throw a pass but then quickly hands off the ball to a running back who was trying to look like he was blocking for the pass. If the quarterback does his job well, the linebackers and other secondary players will drop back into their pass coverage areas and the running back may gain long yardage on the play. Once again the key to success is to make the defense think that you are still doing what you started out doing; then they will react accordingly. A quarterback must work long and hard at it to master the art. Practice and dedication are essential.

KNOWLEDGE OF THE GAME

Good quarterbacks are usually intelligent players. They learn the game thoroughly and become valuable assets to their team. The quarterback's role is to score points for his offensive unit. Understanding the defense—what their strengths and weaknesses are—and knowing

how to avoid their strengths and exploit their weaknesses will give the team a much better chance of scoring. Defensive units like to try to confuse the offense. They will try different tactics, such as linebacker stunts or safety fires, which call for a safety to sneak up toward the line of scrimmage when the ball is about to be snapped and then blitz through the offensive line to get the ball carrier. A smart quarterback must know how to cope with things like that. When linebackers stunt, the quick pass to the receiver who is closest to that linebacker will catch him out of position.

An alert receiver will also see that a safety is creeping up for a fire and should run a pass route into the vacated area to enable the quarterback, also seeing the safety as he scans the defense, to throw a pass to exploit the weakness in the defense. The quarterback must know the down, the distance to the first down marker, the yard line the ball is on, and the time left on the clock at the beginning of every play. All these factors, in addition to many others, must be considered in the huddle in the selection of a play.

It is the quarterback's task to see to it that the game plan is executed to the satisfaction of the coaching staff. If the coach does not call every play from the bench, the quarterback must know the game plan well enough to know what the coach would want called in every situation. Only through close contact with the coach and the strategy to be used to win the game can the quarterback feel qualified to lead his team on the field. He must also recognize his own ability, avoiding the pitfall of thinking that his strong desire to succeed is enough to make the first down when another player's talents give the team a better chance of success. In fact, the quarterback should know the strengths and weaknesses of his own team to avoid bad decisions. He should understand what each play needs for success. If one of his offensive linemen cannot block an opposing lineman, it would not be good judgment to call a crucial play through that hole. Often a wide receiver will come back to the huddle claiming that he can outrun his defender and that a certain pass should be thrown to him. The quarterback must analyze the situation by thinking about the match-up of players and their individual speeds and comparing that to what had actually happened thus far in the game. He may decide that another play has a better chance and thus wait until later when a second and one to go for a first down may give him a chance to waste a play when, even if it fails, the team really won't suffer too much from it.

COMMUNICATION ACTIVITIES

In deciding what to do during the course of a game, the quarterback must take into account the other ten players on the field with him. Each of them is encountering the opponent in different areas of the field, with some match-ups almost amounting to personal wars between an offensive player and his enemy across the line of scrimmage. In these head-to-head combats, one or the other often gets the upper hand. Sometimes it boils down to who has more courage but, more often, it amounts to which player has more strength or better technique. In all cases, a relationship develops that the quarterback should be made aware of and should use in his play selection.

There are only so many plays to be called in a game. Each one should be used wisely to get the most benefit out of it. The quarterback must encourage feedback to him, either before the huddle forms or while the huddle is in session. The quarterback should say something like, "Anybody have an opponent that we can beat?" His teammates must now use their heads, too. As in the case of the wide receiver mentioned earlier, a player should not offer a recommendation to the quarterback unless he is fairly certain it has a good chance of success. This is particularly true when a very important play is needed, perhaps to score a touchdown. Once the quarterback accepts a suggestion and it turns out to be a good one, he is more apt to believe the player in a subsequent situation when an important play comes up.

A great deal of information also comes from the bench, from both the coaches and the other players standing on the sidelines. The coaches

Using a play called by the coach and his spotters, the quarterback hands off to the fullback for a touchdown.

have members of their staff spotting from the top of the grandstands, where a better view of the game can be had. The head coach will ask them to look for specific things like the reaction of the defensive tackles or the type of pass defense coverage being used in the secondary. Any and all information that can be gathered to give insight into how the defense is using its people will make it possible to make adjustments on offense to make better play decisions. It is wise to remember that football games are won through good preparation and a thorough analysis of how to take best advantage of what your opponent is doing. The quarterback must be deeply involved in all the decisions based on what he has learned and what the coaches have learned about the conduct of the game. A decision to be a quarterback carries with it the obligation to be aware of everything going on around you and a commitment to work as hard as you can to meet all the physical and mental requirements of the position.

4 | The Art of Forward Passing

The game of football was played for almost fifty years before the forward pass became popular. Now, more than sixty-five years later, some coaches and teams still use it very sparingly. There are a few reasons for this unusual situation, often expressed in a quote attributed to Woody Hayes, former coach at Ohio State University: "Why don't you throw the ball more often, Woody?" he was asked. He replied, "There are three things that can happen when you throw a pass, and two of them are bad." There is no question that there are risks involved when you throw; but there are also some great rewards, too.

The decision to throw the ball often and to make it a key part of the offense is one that the coach must make. Therefore, if you want to be a quarterback on his team and you want to throw well, you must learn many elements that are involved in developing your technique.

GRIPPING THE BALL

One of the primary steps to be taken in learning to throw is to decide how to place the ball in the throwing hand. If you were to review how all the great passers in history held the ball, you would find that most of them had their own unique style. Probably the main reason for this was the size of their hands. Someone with a large hand can spread his fingers wide and place his index finger near the tip of the ball (but not on it) while his pinky and one or two of his other fingers may be able to rest on the laces. There are many minor variations, but it is enough to say that you have to determine how your hand fits best on the ball to allow you to hold it rather than cradle it. Vary the location of your index finger different distances from the tip of the ball and practice different grips with your ring finger and pinky on the laces. The real test

The quarterback fingers, grasps, raises, and cocks
the ball in the start of his process to throw the ball.

is how many times you can throw a perfect spiral. If you are able to throw eight out of ten spirals, you are getting the knack of it, but you shouldn't stop trying to improve until you can throw almost every one perfectly.

It is important to throw good spirals because a ball that does not spiral well is affected by the wind and will seldom find its mark. A fluttering ball will not get to its destination as quickly as a spiral and will also be more difficult to catch. Its length will be shorter than desired for a long pass because of the increased resistance it will incur when traveling fifty or more yards in the air. Be assured that in order to be accurate and to give yourself the best chance of completing forward passes, you must work constantly on throwing fast, spinning spirals.

THROWING STANCE

Once you have settled how you will hold the ball, the next step is to learn the proper stance, or positioning of your body, to throw the ball effectively. Balance is very important if a ball is going to be thrown well consistently.

When warming up to throw either in practice or in a game, stand with your feet slightly diagonal to the direction in which you are going to throw. Place your feet about shoulder width apart, stand erect, and stride toward your intended receiver. As the ball is moved behind your head when you cock it for the launch, move your head back with it and try to point your chin at the target, too. With your hips turned to face the target and your back arched backward, your midsection will also be pushed forward as you come off your back leg onto your front leg in the passing motion.

FOOTWORK WHILE PASSING

The movement of the feet is very important to the accuracy of a throw. After having arrived at the setup location, the back foot should be planted firmly on the field's surface to establish a firm base to launch the throw. If the surface is natural turf, your shoes' cleats will dig in and give you a solid foot to push off from as you step forward to throw. However, on artificial surfaces you will often find it difficult to plant

With back foot set diagonally, the quarterback takes his step forward to deliver the pass.

the back foot, particularly if the surface is wet. It is important that quarterbacks test the field's surface before a game to become familiar with the conditions with which they will have to cope. Wet fields, for example, usually will not permit as much dependency on the back foot push-off so you may have to rely more on your arm strength to get the ball where you want it.

As stated earlier, when you get to the setup point your feet should be on a slight diagonal. This will allow you to step off the back foot and move your front foot in different degrees of the arc as you seek to lead a receiver with the flight of the ball (see diagram).

QUARTERBACK FOOTWORK THROWING DROP-BACK PASS

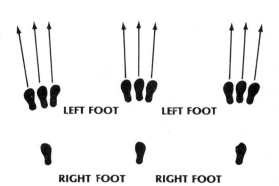

If your back foot is pointed straight at your target, it would be difficult for you to throw to the right of it, since it would require you either to step across the straight line or to force you to push the ball off your right shoulder.

The front foot should always point at the target to which you are throwing or to the spot at which you expect him to be when the ball arrives. Passers who step in one direction and throw to another often have difficulty with their accuracy, sometimes leading to interceptions. The length of the stride of the front leg and foot is also vital to the trajectory of the ball. If you take a long step forward, you will tend to throw the ball low or on a downward course. On the other hand, if you take a short step with the front foot, the ball will often be high in the air when it gets to the target or it will be overthrown, again causing interceptions. The length of the step will vary, depending on the height of the passer. As you throw the ball in practice, pay attention to the length of your stride and make the necessary adjustments. If you start to lose accuracy, throwing the ball either too high or too low, ask the coach or one of the players to look at your stride.

Drop-Back and Setup

When the quarterback takes the ball away from the center at the start of a pass play, it is often referred to as a drop-back action. This term, however, is usually reserved for a pass thrown from a pocket area about seven to nine yards behind the center. It is called a pocket because the pass blocking of the offensive linemen is executed to form a safe area (called a pocket) from which the quarterback may have the time to throw (see diagram). However, there are other types of pass plays besides the drop-back type: the sprint-out, the roll-out, the jump (or quick), and the wide variety of screen passes. Each of these requires different adjustments in the techniques the quarterback uses to take the ball away from the center.

On the drop-back, the quarterback (assuming he throws right-handed) takes his first step back away from the line of scrimmage on his right foot as he pushes off his left foot and makes a half-turn with his body to the right. The first step should be extended as far as the boy's

FORMING THE DROP-BACK PASS POCKET

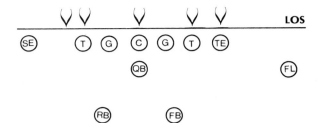

ALIGNMENT AT START OF PASS PLAY

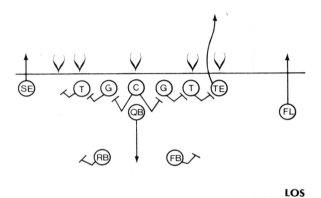

MOVEMENT AFTER BALL IS SNAPPED

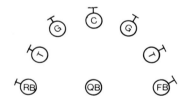

POCKET POSITIONS WHEN BALL IS THROWN

height will allow him to stride comfortably. His body will face the sideline as he moves into his second step, in which the left foot crosses the right foot, with both feet also pointing toward the sideline. This alternating footwork continues for a total of five to seven steps, depending on the distance from the line of scrimmage from which the pass is designed to be thrown and the length of the quarterback's legs and strides.

The drop always stops on the back leg, which is planted firmly to stop the backward motion of the body and to become the base for the start of the throw.

Taking quick, crossing steps, the quarterback drops back to a seven-yard depth to set up to throw a pass.

A sprint-out right with the ball held at the chest, and a sprint-out left with the ball raised to throw.

The sprint-out departure from the center begins much like the open-up step covered in the handoff review. The first step is with the right foot if you are going to the right, with the left foot again serving as the push-off foot to get the body moving quickly. The first step is taken slightly away from the line of scrimmage, at about a 45-degree angle to a distance about five to seven yards deep at a point about even with the right end's position in a tight end formation (see diagram below left).

The purpose of this action is to put pressure on the defense's left side, who must play the sprint-out as either a run or a pass play. When the quarterback decides that he will throw, he must cock the ball as he steps on his left foot and throw it as his right foot carries his body's weight, while running. This kind of setup is done in stride and not from a standing, set position as in the drop-back.

The roll-out drop is usually different while you are coming away from the center but becomes the same as the sprint-out at the time of delivery. Many coaches prefer to have the quarterback start in the same manner as a reverse pivot, turning to the left starting off with the left foot and spinning on the right foot. The angle into the right side of the backfield area ends up being the same as that of the sprint-out and requires the same moving setup and throw.

Screen passes may be thrown out of the back-drop, sprint-out, or roll-out except that on the drop-back, you usually must stop at the normal

The quarterback rolls out and may either pass or run, depending on how the defense covers him and the receivers.

setup area and then retreat another five or more yards to lead the onrushing defenders farther away from the back who is going to receive the pass (see diagram below right).

Screen passes require deception on the part of most of the offensive unit. While the quarterback is doing his thing on his drop-back motion, he must also *eye fake* the defense into

SPRINT-OUT PASS FOOTWORK

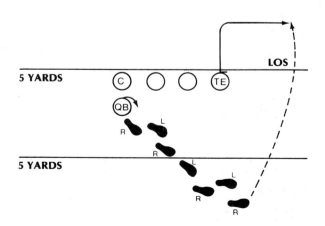

PRO-RIGHT–SCREEN LEFT

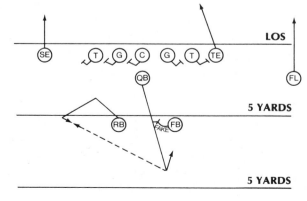

thinking that he is going to throw the ball in a different direction. Eye faking means that the quarterback must look away from the would-be receiver to let the defense think he is throwing it elsewhere. As he does this, he must continue to retreat as though he can't make up his mind where to throw the ball.

Sprint-out and roll-out screen passes usually only require the quarterback to stop and throw the ball back in the opposite direction. The screen is set on the left side if the quarterback movement is to the right. The pass arc and velocity are the same in all cases. The ball must be thrown softly and high to get over the defensive linemen who will try to block or intercept it and to enable the receiver to run under it and catch it easily.

The jump or quick pass is most often thrown with little or no retreat from the center. If it is thrown to a tight end over the middle or straight out, the quarterback must stand right up after getting the ball and throw it as quickly as possible, or as soon as his receiver is open. Some quick passes are thrown out toward the sideline to a wide receiver. The quarterback must turn in that direction, step slightly away from the line of scrimmage as he sets up to throw, and fire the ball quickly. Other quick passes are not thrown until a fake is made to a running back who is diving into the line. Then the quarterback stands up and throws the ball.

BODY, ARM, AND WRIST COORDINATION

It is necessary for you to get your body totally coordinated in order to become a good passer. After the grip, stance, and footwork have been stabilized, your upper body, primarily the arms and wrist of your throwing arm, have to assume full responsibility for the quality of your throw. "Practice, practice, practice" is an oft-heard expression on the football field, and never was it more true.

When you get to the setup point, and you have planted your back foot, the ball should be at your chest level and you should have both hands on it. When you see the target, you must quickly use the nonthrowing arm and hand to push the ball up over your throwing shoulder as your throwing hand and arm take over the control of the ball. The throwing arm should then cock the ball behind your ear with the tip of the ball pointing at the sky. When you begin the forward stride with your front foot, your backward body arch should start forward with the throwing arm. Your wrist should now start to uncoil from its coiled position cocked behind your ear, and you should start pulling your throwing arm down.

At the start of the throwing arc, your elbow, which was pointing at the target when your arm was cocked, now starts to unflex so that your

The ball is cocked behind the ear with the point of the ball pointing straight up as the quarterback launches the start of the pass.

As the ball comes forward over the top of his head, the quarterback pulls the ball down and forward to give it the velocity he needs to throw the pass.

arm is fully extended when the ball is held at its highest point in the delivery arc. At this point, your wrist and hand should be pulling the ball down and forward to launch it into flight as your fingers slide off the ball, causing it to spiral.

THROWING TECHNIQUES FOR DIFFERENT PASSES

The actual delivery of the ball takes it from its cocked position to its release from the fingers. But the term delivery also involves how the ball is thrown, with distance and velocity in mind. The basic throwing motion is the same, regardless of the kind of pass being thrown. But adjustments have to be made in the delivery of the ball to give each type of pass a good chance of success.

There are many kinds of passes. There are long passes, short passes, out and in passes, and screen or flare passes. Within each category are many different versions. For example, a long pass could be a fly, flag, zig, post, and on and on. To the quarterback, a long pass means that he is going to have to make a slight adjustment in the way he throws the ball.

First of all, a long pass means that it will take longer for the receiver to run downfield and get open to receive the ball. Therefore, the quarterback should take a deeper drop before he sets up to throw the ball. Practice should have determined how far the quarterback can throw and how fast the receiver is racing downfield. When the quarterback determines that it is time to throw the ball, he must reach back a little farther when he starts to launch the ball and must throw it on a high trajectory to enable it to travel farther down the field. A long pass thrown high will also give the receiver an opportunity to run under it if it is thrown inaccurately. Long passes also usually force the quarterback to throw the ball as far as he can if he waits too long to throw it. The rule to follow is: throw the ball as soon as you see that the receiver will be open; don't wait until he is open, or he may run out of your range.

A short pass may be thrown on a low trajectory because you want it to get to its destination quickly and your accuracy over a shorter distance should be good to excellent. The ball must also be thrown hard with great speed or velocity to increase the chances of completing it. The longer the ball is in the air, the greater the opportunity for the defense to intercept it or knock it down. There is also an anticipation factor in short passes. The quarterback must not wait until the receiver is open and waiting for the ball; he must throw the ball before that to a spot at which he expects the receiver to be after running his pass route. There is a split second when the receiver's fake has allowed him to get some distance away from his defender in order to be free to catch the ball. The ball must be on its way at that instant, so the quarterback must anticipate that moment and must fire the ball as hard as he can.

Out passes, or sideline passes as some of them are called, require a quarterback with a very strong arm and an ability to throw the ball with great speed. When executed properly, the out pass is one of the highest-percentage pass plays that can be used. Usually, a wide receiver is covered by one defender out in the flat area. That defender has to be certain not to allow the fleet receiver to get past or behind him because,

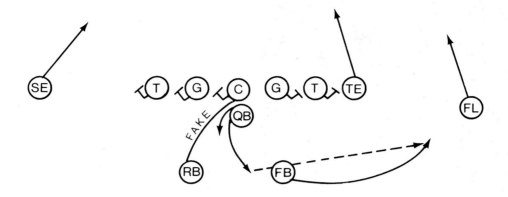

PRO-RIGHT–FLARE RIGHT

if a long pass is completed to him, it is almost certainly going to be a touchdown. Therefore, he will often play five to seven yards off the line of scrimmage to make it more difficult for the receiver to get past him. By playing off that far, he is inviting the offense to use the out pattern. All that is necessary after that is for the receiver to run a quick out pattern about five yards downfield and for the quarterback to gun the ball there in time for the receiver to catch it as soon as he makes his fake and steps toward the sideline.

Screen and flare passes are thrown in similar fashion. In both cases, a back will be running under them, often with his back partially toward the quarterback (see diagram). By lofting the ball and throwing it as softly as the distance will allow, the quarterback not only gives the back a better chance to catch it, but he is also making it more difficult for an opposing lineman to knock it down. The real danger in this kind of play is that the longer the ball stays in the air, the greater the chance that any unseen player may also have an opportunity to run under it and intercept it. The quarterback must look very carefully to avoid that, because an interception on this kind of pass often leads to a long touchdown run.

Without going into all the many different kinds of passes, the conclusion is that there is one adjustment or another that must be made for a pass to be thrown correctly. Practice sessions between quarterbacks and receivers should point up the best way to make those adjustments and provide the timing that is so necessary to a successful passing attack.

DELIVERY AND FOLLOW-THROUGH

Delivery also means the throwing form used by the quarterback as he prepares to throw the ball. As we have just seen, the quarterback must react somewhat differently on various types of pass plays. On some of them he may drop back quickly and deliver a soft pass out in the flat to a running back running a flare pattern. Here again, he should try to eye fake the defense away from the receiver. As soon as he has completed the throw, he should run after the pass to cover against a possible interception. The delivery on this play would require finesse, normal timing, and a cautious follow-up.

On a post pattern, which calls for a receiver to split the seam between two safety zones at a distance of about thirteen yards, the quarterback's delivery must be as precise as pos-

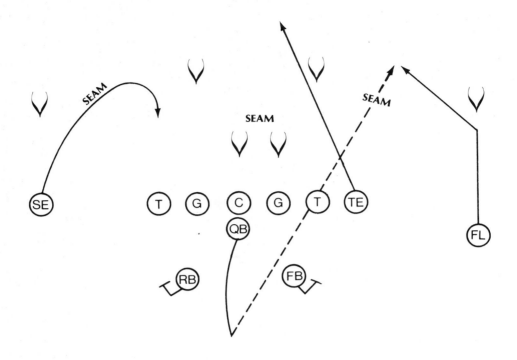

PRO-RIGHT–FLANKER POST

sible in both his drop-back distance and the speed with which he sets up and delivers the ball. This kind of pass, as well as many others set for specific places in the secondary, requires the quarterback to fire the ball and follow through with his delivery, much like a pitcher throwing a fastball at the other team's home run hitter (see diagram).

The follow-through motion begins at the moment the ball leaves the quarterback's fingers with all the weight on his front leg, his back leg up in the air, and his throwing arm swinging low under his body with the thumb of the throwing hand pointing at the ground. It is the finishing touch to the art of throwing a football. If it is not learned and done well, a quarterback will never become an effective passer. It is as important to the quality of a pass as any of the other aspects of throwing the ball.

Training to Develop Skills

Anything that you do properly that is repeated often enough will result in improvement. The key to that statement is that it must be done properly. Your coach will want to advise you on each of your techniques and will suggest methods for improvement. Follow his guidance and dedicate yourself to meeting the standards that he sets for you.

Our recommendations are more general. We feel that a quarterback must make basic improvements in a number of areas if his local team is going to benefit from having him as its quarterback.

First, there are many ways to strengthen your throwing arm. Throw the ball as often as you can, even if it is just in your backyard with someone able to catch it and return it to you.

The follow-through motion starts when the ball leaves the quarterback's fingers and his weight shifts from the back to the front foot, and his hand turns counterclockwise.

This will help you perfect your accuracy and the consistency of your spirals.

Second, use small barbells in a wide variety of ways to build the strength of your arm muscles. In particular, move a two-pound bell in the same motion that your arm will move as it takes the ball from behind your ear through its upward arc. Finger grips will also do wonders for the strength of your fingers, hands, wrists, and forearms.

Next, do some of the following drills to build up your throwing ability. Kneel down on your left leg, put the ball behind your ear, and throw the ball ten, fifteen, twenty, and twenty-five yards to another quarterback who can return it to you in the same manner. Then do the same thing with only the right knee down. Afterward, put both knees down, and soon you will see that a great deal of effort is required of your upper body and arms to propel the ball the longer distances. Done regularly, it will strengthen your throwing arm immensely.

Another good drill involves hanging an old tire on a rope from the branch of a tree and throwing at it from varying distances. Once you have become consistent enough with the tire hanging motionless, have someone swing it from side to side like a pendulum. This will help you develop your ability to hit a moving target, which is so necessary to leading a receiver with your pass to enable him to catch it without breaking stride.

To improve your footwork and body rhythm, become an expert at jumping rope. It will not only make you quicker on your feet but will also increase your speed and strengthen your legs. Remember that your legs are vital to your throwing ability, both to get you to the setup area quickly and to launch your passes on the sprint-out and roll-out types of passes.

Running backward is probably one of the least appreciated ways of improving coordination and body balance, two very important qualities a passing quarterback must have. Do it with a group of your friends or do it alone, but be sure to include it in your plans. Another effective way to build up your hands and arms is to do fingertip push-ups. Do your push-ups the regular way, but do not let the palms of your hands touch the floor. They do not have to be done quickly but should be held for as long as you can.

Most teams now have plastic tubes or stretch ropes through which to run high-step drills, and they have been largely responsible for the vast improvement in agility in football over the last ten years. They develop quick feet, nimble legs, and better body control, all of which are necessary for a quarterback. If you don't have a setup like this, arrange some old tires in a staggered manner and run through and around them in many different ways (see diagram). Do all of these things to get yourself ready and then look forward to enjoying yourself when you perform all of the quarterback's required duties on the field in the best way you can.

NUMBERS INDICATE LEFT FOOT–RIGHT FOOT

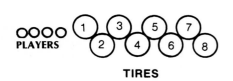

TIRES

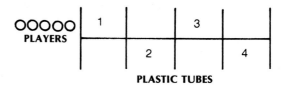

PLASTIC TUBES

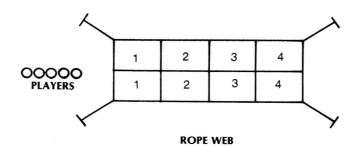

ROPE WEB

5 | Keys to Good Play Calling

Earlier we briefly covered the importance of an offensive game plan. It should be based on two broad factors: what the team is able to do well and what the opponent's apparent weaknesses are. Both of these subjects are covered in much detail by a coaching staff while getting ready for an upcoming game. The quarterback must be on top of it all if he is going to be able to serve his team well.

UNDERSTANDING THE OFFENSE

The things your team does well stem from what the coach thinks is important in his offensive scheme. He may lean more toward running with the ball and only throw when his running game is faltering, or he may believe in using the pass as a surprise weapon. On the other hand, he may be a coach who will only run the ball enough to keep the defense honest and in their rush-oriented defensive alignments and who then uses the pass as effectively as he can.

After the team is put together early in the year, the preseason practice routine always includes some full team scrimmages, either intrasquad or against some other teams. Often they are played under game conditions, with officials present and with first-down chains to simulate a real contest. It is during these sessions that the coach and the players as well begin to understand what the team's strengths are that should become the mainstays of the offense. It may be that the team has some effective offensive linemen who are able to move people out of the way to open holes through which to run. Or it may be that there is a strong running back who surprised everyone with his hard running and elusiveness. Perhaps there is a wide receiver who constantly gets away from his defender and can catch the ball and run well with it, too. And, of course, there may be a quarterback who not only executes well and throws well but also provides a spark to the team and leads them to bigger and better things. All of these things and many others are reviewed by the coaching staff to lay the plans for the season.

The coach then decides what he wants to do and begins to firm up specific plays that he feels will use these strengths, and the long practice sessions begin. As the quarterback, you will soon be well aware of what the coach wants to do as you prepare for the first game. The first pregame week is now at hand.

PREGAME OFFENSIVE PLAN

It is not always possible to scout your first game opponent unless he has played the week before. If not, you will have to make certain decisions about what they are likely to do based on last year's team, what they did against your team and against other teams on their schedule. There will always be a doubt in your mind as to whether they have made some changes with this year's team that could foul up your plans, but you have no way of predicting that. It may force you to make adjustments early in the game, so be prepared for it.

The most important things to know about the other team are the talents of their players and the defensive formations and tactics they like to use. If you have solid information in both of these areas, you can make your plans accordingly. For example, if one of their defensive tackles is almost impossible to block, the game plan will include running to the opposite side of the line or may call for a variety of trap plays to attack him by surprise rather than head on. Perhaps your outstanding offensive tackle will be playing opposite a defender who rises up as he crosses the line of scrimmage, thereby exposing his entire body for solid shoulder blocks. You can be sure the coach will want to hit his area often. You should look for that to develop because a short yardage play for a first down may suggest that you run that hole.

Always look for weak players in the secondary because if you can attack that vulnerable area it may lead to an easy touchdown. How do your receivers match up with the people who will be covering them? Their safety may be a great tackler, but perhaps he doesn't have as much speed as your flanker.

Every defensive formation has its strong points and weak areas. By matching their personnel to their formations, you may find other areas to exploit. The coach may want to add some man-in-motion plays because he may see a problem in their defense that would make it difficult for them to cover it well. The coach may also want to adjust some of your basic plays to hit their weaknesses. For example, the other team's coach may believe in having his down linemen play directly on the heads of the offensive linemen. Your coach may direct your guards and tackles to open up their line splits to force the opponents even wider apart to make for wider holes in the inside running game. It is always important to see how a team defends against the end sweep, particularly if you have a fast running back who can fly around the corner. There are dozens of other factors that go into the creation of a game plan, and the coach will want you to know it through and through, especially if he lets you call the plays.

INTERFACE WITH THE COACHES

When the game begins and you start by following the game plan to the letter, certain phases of it will work as well as you had expected them to and others will be marginally or completely unsuccessful. As the game progresses, you must try to determine why certain plays failed, to evoke a decision to modify them, scrap them, or try them again.

The proper approach is to consult the coaching staff and get their thoughts and ideas on the play. There may be some information from the spotting crew that will explain why the play didn't work. It may be that the defense happened to do something unusual on that play or that one of the linemen missed a block. It could also be that everyone did the best he could, but the other team outplayed you. The coaches are responsible for changes in the game plan, so give them the first opportunity to advise you.

COMMUNICATION WITH THE PLAYERS

After getting the coaches' views on your lack of success, you should also try to feel out your teammates as to their points of view. You may hear about something that the coaching staff missed from their vantage point. Perhaps the defensive lineman was holding an offensive man, making it impossible to block him out of the hole. It may have been a slant stunt in which the defender charged diagonally across the line of scrimmage, taking your man by surprise. Little things like these can cause a play to fail, but when you call it again later it may lead to a big gain.

All players should try to identify the tendencies of their opponents as the game goes on. Some down linemen like to vary the way they try to penetrate an offense, often based on the down and distance to go for a first down. For example, on third and long, when a pass play is usually anticipated, a defensive tackle may take a higher stance and try to pass-rush to the outside of the offensive tackle. This is a typical defensive tackle tactic. The offensive tackle should pass that information on to the quarterback because it would give a draw play a better chance of success and the quarterback may want to try it on the next occasion.

LOOKING FOR DEFENSIVE WEAKNESSES

In the course of a game the defensive units are likely to change their formations to cope with what you are doing well against them. They may rearrange their personnel in very subtle ways that will hardly be noticeable unless you and your team are looking for them. This situation may lead to the failure of a play that had worked very well in the beginning but is now being stopped repeatedly.

Once again, the coaches and the players must be questioned about why it is happening and what to do to cope with it. As the quarterback, you are often in the best position to observe the reaction of the defense as you stand behind the center, waiting to call the snap sounds prior to the snapping of the ball. This is often the time that the defense will do something to try to confuse your offensive people. For example, the

defensive front may all slide to their left or right to put themselves in different alignments with your offensive front. This can often result in confusion in the blocking assignments. It is not uncommon to see two men blocking one defender while another defender gets into your backfield without anyone laying a hand on him. Blocking rules are established to cope with this kind of action, but someone may blow an assignment.

The most frequently used defensive adjustment is the linebacker stunt or blitz, as it is sometimes called. When the snap sounds are being called, one or two or all of the linebackers may be going in between two of their down linemen in the hope that they can get into your backfield and break up your play. Here again there are blocking rules, but even though your people may know what to do, they may fail to keep their people out of your midst. Game plans often call for the tight end to release quickly into an area vacated by a stunting linebacker to catch a quick pass from the quarterback who is retreating off the line of scrimmage as fast as he can to throw the ball before he is tackled by a defender.

When you see changes being made, consult with your coach at the earliest opportunity and get his direction as to what to do about them. Make sure your offensive unit knows what the changes are, even if it is just a few words as you call a play in the huddle or on the way back to the next huddle.

USING YOUR TEAM'S STRENGTHS

There is a familiar saying in football circles: "If you're doing something well, keep doing it until they take it away from you." This generally applies to offensive success that you may be having in a game when something you are doing just keeps producing results, time after time. It may be any pass play to one of your receivers who just keeps on beating his defender. Or it may be a draw play that the defense has just not been able to figure out and it keeps getting big yardage for you.

There are some football people who feel that you should save some of these sure things for crucial plays when you must make yardage, but we don't hold with that philosophy. You must remember that there are just so many chances that your team will get during a game, and it is your job to make the most of those chances. Perhaps there is a weak down lineman who is causing your opponent most of his trouble. You may want to use different plays to get to his area on the line of scrimmage, but it really doesn't make too much sense to ignore a real weak spot in their armor. Until the game is virtually wrapped up, the quarterback's role is to put points on the scoreboard. Be well aware of what your good plays are and which of your personnel are producing the best results. Your analysis can be the key to success.

THE USE OF AUDIBLES AND SNAP SOUNDS

Anyone who wants to be a success at the quarterback position must learn to use audibles. This is the technique used at the line of scrimmage when the quarterback, who is about to start the snap sounds to begin the play, sees something in the defensive alignment that he wants to take advantage of and doesn't want to wait until the next play. In order to do this, he must be able to use one of many different techniques available to change the play at the line of scrimmage. To explain this thoroughly, let's begin with the use of snap sounds and the other

things a quarterback says when he is poised behind the center at the start of each play.

The huddle is the area from which every offensive play begins. The quarterback calls the play, usually repeats it to make sure that everyone has heard him, then announces the snap sound on which the ball will be centered. He then shouts, "Break," and the team heads for the line of scrimmage. When all the players are properly positioned, the quarterback says, "Get down," and everyone gets into his respective offensive stance. He then says, "Roll it" to signify that the next sound out of his mouth is the first snap sound. If he had called the snap on the first sound in the huddle, then the first sound after "Roll it" would cause the center to snap the ball.

Some coaches prefer to have the snap sounds be rhythmic and require their quarterbacks to repeat them with consistent timing. On the other hand, tests have been conducted that tend to support nonrhythmic sounds to achieve the best results in getting everyone to start at the same time. The tests indicated that if you have to wait to hear the next sound, you will be poised ready to move when you hear it rather than to anticipate when the beat of the quarterback's rhythm really is.

Our technique has been to use the word "Go" as the snap sound. If the snap sound given in the huddle was the second sound, then the quar-

The quarterback looks for a weakness in the defense before calling an audible to change the play at the line of scrimmage.

terback would say, "go . . . go," and the ball would be brought up to him by the center. Constant practice, starting from early in the preseason, will get everyone accustomed to the technique, and very little trouble will be encountered. You will also probably find that the entire team is getting off together, a vital part of the offensive arsenal.

Most coaches use numbers to designate their plays. Usually the first number refers to the formation, the second to the ball carrier, and the third to the area or hole through which the ball will go. It is through the use of these numbers that most audibles are employed.

Let's go through a typical application of an audible. Before a game, the coach will designate which plays he would like to use as audibles in certain situations. With that in mind, the quarterback and the entire offense will have an idea as to what may be used later in the game. Everyone must be alert to the use of them in order to make full use of the system.

If the quarterback were to call a play known as *128*—the 1 formation (pro-set), the 2 back (the left halfback) running through the 8 hole (the gap between the right guard and the right tackle)—and came out of the huddle to find that the defense had overloaded that area, he would want to check off the play to another play (call an audible) that would give the team a better chance to gain yardage. Here is the way he would do it.

After he had directed everyone to get into his offensive stance by saying "Get down," and before he said "Roll it," he would say "One." By repeating the first number of the offensive

play called in the huddle he would be telling the other ten players that he was about to change the play. He might then say, "Twenty-seven," which is the same play as the twenty-eight except that it is to the other side of the center between the left guard and left tackle.

As soon as his teammates hear the new play number, they wait for the quarterback to say "Roll it" and for him to call the snap sounds that were given in the huddle. They all take off together on the snap of the ball to run a 127 play instead of a 128.

Deciding which play to switch off to is often a difficult task for a young quarterback. His choice must be based on what he thinks is a more vulnerable area and what the coach has prepared the team to use. It requires a great deal of poise for a youngster to stand calmly behind the center and display his coolness and understanding of the game.

In particular, the quarterback must also be an actor; he must be able to announce what appear to be audibles but are really techniques to further confuse the defense. This may be done by using a fake formation number after saying "Get down," which would make the defense think he was changing the play. In the above example, instead of saying "One," he might say "Two" or some other number. His teammates would know that it wasn't the formation number called in the huddle, but the defense would never know and they might start scurrying around to try to confuse the offense to their own disadvantage. A quarterback who can handle audibles is a big asset to his team. It gives them another dimension with which to score.

6 | Running Backs—Skills and Techniques

HOW TO CHOOSE A RUNNING BACK

Probably the second most important skill position to fill after the quarterback is that of the running back. This is the position that earns the yardage the hard way, over land rather than in the air. It requires many important qualities in an athlete, some of which are identical to those of a quarterback.

Once again, the importance of physical coordination comes to the forefront. Full body control is required in order to carry a football and run effectively. This is true because a running back has to twist, turn, and thrust his body to avoid tackles in a crowd or in an open field.

When the coaches time the speed of their players, those with good times in the forty-yard sprint should be the first ones considered as running backs. The next feature to look for is the strength and ruggedness of the muscular build. Boys with compact muscular development will be more able to withstand the contact that a running back must endure and will probably be stronger to break tackles when hit by defenders.

PHYSICAL REQUIREMENTS

Players who have either developed their bodies naturally or used a weights program to build themselves up are going to be attractive to a coach looking for running backs. They should be of at least average size for the level of ball they are playing, taller if they are heavier than average and shorter if they are lighter. In general, tall, thin boys do not make good running backs, nor do short, heavy boys.

If boys are tall, they should be well developed because they have a greater area that can be hit.

Shorter boys are often attractive because they are usually quick, and if their frames are strong enough to cope with the stress placed on them when they are tackled, they can often make a big contribution to the team.

It is extremely vital for a running back to have good balance because he will frequently be hit and knocked off balance. The ability to recover balance can make the difference between an average running back and a good running back. A coach can usually assess a boy's balance by observing the way he runs. Many players run with their bodies under full control, which allows them to cut sharply and change direction. Inability to make sharp turns without losing your balance is an indicator that you need improvement in this skill.

There is a definite rhythm to a well-coordinated athlete's running ability. He moves his arms in perfect unison with his legs, and his body leans forward, biting into the wind and providing the best speed his powerful legs will give him. The coach will recognize those who have put their entire running stride together with good timing and control.

How to Handle the Ball

The handling of the ball falls into two general categories: the first is the receipt of the ball, either on a handoff or on a pitch from the quarterback; the second is the control and movement of the ball when you run with it. One is as important as the other because a failure to do both consistently and well will make you a

A quick, rugged running back cuts sharply into a hole and turns upfield to gain yardage.

greater liability to the team, rather than an asset.

The handoff from the quarterback or another running back on a reverse requires good positioning of the body and the hands and arms. The running back must try to get his body as close to the quarterback as possible to obtain many benefits. First, when the ball is not extended into a distance, it is more difficult for the defenders to see the ball and the deception is enhanced. Second, with both players moving in different directions, there is a need for hand-to-eye coordination so they can both see where the ball is and where it is going. The quarterback tries to put it firmly but gently into the running back's soft diaphram area just above the belt, and the running back tries to grasp it with both hands to pull it into his body. Whereas the

The running back gets close to the quarterback for the handoff and raises his near arm to accept the ball.

quarterback's eyes focus directly on the running back's body, the running back must keep his eyes on the area he is running toward, but his peripheral vision must pick up the ball when the quarterback presses it into his upper midsection.

Next, it is important that the bodies don't collide. They may brush up against each other, but a bumping motion often causes a fumble and these must be avoided at all cost. The thrust here is that although the bodies must be close, they should not be too close to cause any kind of jarring contact. There is also concern for the split second when both bodies are departing from each other and the quarterback is removing his hand while the running back is pulling the ball into his body.

The best way to cope with this condition is to have the running back hold up his elbow on the quarterback's side to create an opening through which the ball can be handed and for the quarterback to remove his hand after the handoff. This technique is also good for the fake handoffs because the running back can raise his elbow to make the defense think he is getting the ball. This is most often seen on play action passes when the quarterback wants to freeze the linebackers by letting them think the running

The running back follows the flight of the ball from the quarterback and looks it into his hands.

back is getting the ball, thereby releasing the tight end over the middle for a quick pass.

The pitch from the quarterback has a number of phases that must be learned well. The running back should take off from his starting position and head in the direction of the play. Some coaches ask that they start off at full speed, while others ask for about three-quarters speed until the ball is received by the running back's hands. In either case, the running back must look for the flight of the ball as soon as he takes off and follow the flight until he "looks it" into his hands. This expression means exactly what it says and is used frequently for any player who must catch the football. The running back must actually follow the ball's flight and watch it hit his fingers and hands. This almost guarantees that a fumble will not occur. Instant replay on TV has proven that when apparently easy catches are missed, they are often the result of the receiver taking his eyes off the ball too soon. When the running back catches the pitch from the quarterback, he must tuck it away under the arm that is away from the middle of the field.

Knowing which arm should carry the ball is a problem to some running backs because they never took the time to learn a simple basic rule: if you're running to the right, carry with the right; if you're running to the left, carry with the left. The basis for this rule is simple. If you hold the ball in your right arm as you go around the right end, your left arm will be available for a straight arm. The use of the straight arm is one of the most important weapons a running back has and is all too often ignored or precluded by use of the wrong arm to hold the ball.

FOOTWORK REQUIREMENTS—STANCE AND STEPS

Knowing how to use your feet is another skill that you must possess to be a successful running back. The first involvement of the feet comes in your stance. The coach will tell you where in the backfield he wants you to take your stance. When you arrive there, place your feet shoulder width apart and adjust the toe of your back foot so that it is parallel to the instep of the front foot. If you are right-handed, the back foot is the right foot.

Then lower your body to a crouch position until the fingers of your right hand, fully extended downward, touch the surface of the field. This amounts to a forward leaning stance in which your legs will not be bent very far and that will allow your back to be parallel to the ground. As your right arm hangs directly down from the right shoulder, the left elbow should be placed on top of the left thigh with the left hand hanging down between the legs.

When you raise your rump to a height that will make your back parallel to the ground, the heel of your right foot will come an inch or so off the ground. This will tend to shift your body weight forward on the right hand so the left foot must relieve some of the pressure to avoid having the right hand bear some of the weight. A smart coach will pull out the right arm of running backs in their stances to see if they are keeping the proper balance. If the back falls forward when he does it, then too much weight is on the right hand. Stances must be observed at all times during the season to make certain that they are still correct.

Starting steps are easily taken in all directions from this stance. When running to the right, the feet should be turned to the right as the first step is taken with the right foot. This short step should be followed quickly by a longer crossover step with the left foot as it crosses the right foot. A run to the left is exactly opposite, with the left foot taking the first short step and the right crossing over. In addition, both arms should be used to swing the body in the direction you are

Two running backs take their stances—the front running back in a three-point and the rear running back in a two-point stance.

going to help turn the body and the feet together. They should then begin pumping to accelerate your running speed so you will get to the point the ball will be handed off or pitched by the quarterback. On runs straight ahead, the first step should be taken with the left foot with the back foot thrusting the body forward. A slanting, diagonal run to the right should begin with the right foot, and a similar run to the left should use the left foot. Again the arms should begin to churn right away to help get the legs moving at the same pace. Start-up speed is one of the most important qualities a coach looks for in a running back because it helps them get to the line of scrimmage quickly. This helps the offensive linemen because they don't have to

The running backs take their first steps with their left foot to move quickly toward the line of scrimmage.

hold their blocks too long on a direct run into the line. Quick speed also increases the hitting force a back has when he is running through a crowd and has to rely on breaking some tackles in order to gain yardage. In this area of play, a running back is better off taking short controlled steps, going into his longer, natural stride only when he gets clear of the line of scrimmage. The reasons for the short steps are that they increase balance and body control and allow the running back to regain control of his momentum when he is hit a glancing blow. It also permits better release of the running back's strength and power because he is pushing quickly with one foot and then the other.

Once the running back has gone through the crowd he can turn on his full speed, as long as he can still quickly put on the reins when he is approaching another tackler. It is far more difficult to change direction at full speed.

RUNNING TECHNIQUES FOR SUCCESS

Body lean is a term used very frequently in football circles. It refers to the angle of the body as a ball carrier runs with the ball. It also implies that if the running back's body is leaning forward, then at contact he will probably fall forward and thereby gain extra yardage. Although this is often true, the real reason for this technique is to allow the running back to deliver a blow to the defender who attempts to tackle him, in effect to make him far more difficult to tackle by keeping his center of gravity low and by reducing the amount of body surface exposed for the tackler to hit.

It is also true that, by keeping a low center of gravity, the running back is capable of keeping his balance far better than if he were more erect. The best way to picture this is to think of the running back as a rubber ball that is capable of bouncing off one tackler and regaining his balance in time to bounce off another tackler without getting knocked off his feet.

In addition to power running in a crowd, the running back must be able to fake (or juke, as some coaches say) a tackler into missing him in a one-on-one situation. This can be done only when a running back runs under control and is capable of changing direction. The best tech-

The hole opens and the running back turns on his speed and darts through the daylight for big yardage.

The running back runs under control and prepares to cut sharply between two defenders to get free.

nique is to take a step at the tackler, try to stop your forward thrust, and shift it to one side or the other of the tackler. While doing this you should try to keep the ball away from him to permit you to straight arm with the free arm. By pushing his head away with your straight arm and shifting your weight and direction away from him, you should be able to avert a tackle.

Another technique seen in most great runners is the ability to spin and turn your body as you are in the process of trying to free yourself from a tackler. Once again, you should step at him and straight arm, but as you do you must now turn your body completely around, with your legs churning as you do. The push-off with the straight arm can help you turn, but the main effort should be placed on your feet and legs. When you take that step at him, twist on it and push yourself around with the other foot, using your arms to help spin your body. This is a great talent to have and can be developed as part of the running drills.

How to Be a Smart Running Back

There are many ways in which a running back can increase his value to his team, some by using his head and others using his body. Let's take a look at each of them.

Every player has to evaluate himself to determine what his good qualities are and which areas need improvement. For example, if a running back has trouble breaking tackles, he should work on building his overall strength, particularly in his upper body. He should then try to develop a forearm shiver technique that is

With his fingers covering the tip of the ball, the running back can help prevent costly fumbles.

used when a tackler makes contact by thrusting the free arm upward with the forearm. By combining it with a juke or a spin, the running back can often free himself and gain more yardage.

There are occasions when a running back suddenly begins to fumble the ball more frequently than before. He should then decide that steps must be taken to reverse this trend. This can be done by holding both arms around the ball with a hand on either end. Because it is difficult to run fast while holding the ball in that fashion, as soon as he clears the line of scrimmage he can move it to one arm or the other, depending on which sideline he turns to to run toward. In addition, when he sees that he is about to be tackled he should pull the ball into his armpit and bring the other hand over to help hold on to it. The only time he should run with it out on his forearm is when he is in an open field with no one about to tackle him. Fumbling is often nothing more than carelessness and can be avoided by a smart running back.

As stated earlier, the coach will tell you where to start from on every play. However, it may be necessary for you to cheat a little in one direction or another, depending on the type of play called. For example, if you are getting to the line of scrimmage too slowly and the hole is closing before you get there, you may want to line up about six inches to a foot closer to the line of scrimmage and get there sooner. Be sure to advise the quarterback that you will be doing it so he is ready to hand off sooner. There are many other plays in which this kind of thing can be done. Draw plays and trap plays are important insofar as timing is concerned. A slight adjustment may make the difference between a successful play and a failure.

Never let the defense know where you are headed when you are in your starting stance. Some running backs have a bad habit of looking in the direction of the hole, and a smart linebacker often picks up this signal. Always look straight ahead until the quarterback has handed you the ball. Then look for daylight and veer off in the direction of a hole. It may not be where it was supposed to be, but a smart running back will look for the nearest one to the original hole area and get through it as fast as he can.

By holding both hands on the ball, the running back can protect it from defenders' hands when running in a crowd.

When the running back breaks into the secondary, he can swing the ball freely in one hand but must pull it in when he is about to be tackled.

TRAINING TO DEVELOP SKILLS

A running back's main skills are running, blocking, and catching the football. You can improve your running speed by building up your legs and by improving your starting stance. Try to develop a style of running, aided by your pumping arms, that is best suited to your body build and your natural striding ability. If you are a long strider, work on shortening your stride by taking shorter steps. Have your speed timed frequently to see if you are making some improvement. Ask the coach or a teammate to watch you come out of your stance to see if you are pushing off well and to determine whether you are taking too short or too long a stride. Do it with someone calling snap sounds so that you may simulate game conditions.

Blocking ability can be improved by practice and sound instruction. Your coach will explain that you must get your shoulder into a defender without losing your feet. And once you have made contact, you must keep your legs driving until you hear the play-ending whistle. Pass blocking calls for you to take a semisquat position, as though you were imitating an ape, and then wait until the defender is practically on you to thrust up and through his chest to take away his charge. Once you have popped him, recover, squat, and pop him again. The technique is easy, but you will have to practice it to perfect it.

Open field blocking requires a cross body block. Run under control until you get a few feet away from your opponent. Then try to throw your body across his thighs and roll through him. The part of your body that should make contact is your upper thigh and hip. Extend your arms and legs to lengthen your blocking surface to guarantee making contact in case he should try to sidestep your blocking approach. Do not dive at him from afar because you will almost surely miss him. Also be certain not to make contact with him at any place on his body between the side of his knee and his back. That's how clips are thrown and a good player keeps them to a minimum. It is better not to block at all if you think that it is going to be a clip block. The team can do without the fifteen-yard penalty.

Running back blocks from a semisquat position to give the quarterback time to throw a quick pass.

Two running backs lead ball carrier around end and prepare to throw cross body downfield blocks.

Catching ability should also be worked on constantly to make it as good as everything else you do. The following chapter, on wide receivers, will go into a great deal of detail to explain how to catch a football. The running back must also be concerned with the position of his body because many passes in the backfield are not more than a few yards away and the running back must turn at the right time and in the right way to make it easier for the quarterback to get the ball to him (see diagram).

On swing and flare passes the running back must run an arc pattern to be sure to have his body turned enough so that he may see the ball coming to him. On out and circle patterns he must find a way to get through the crowds at the line of scrimmage before he begins his pattern. This is often possible if the running back tries to avoid contact with defenders by not running too fast in that area. Then, as soon as possible, the head should be turned to look for the ball because the quarterback may be in a rush to throw it. Remember, if you're a running back on a pass route, the quarterback often has one less player blocking for him and may be under pressure.

TYPICAL RUNNING BACK PASS ROUTES

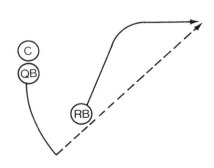

RUNNING BACK OUT PASS

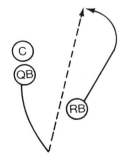

RUNNING BACK CIRCLE PASS

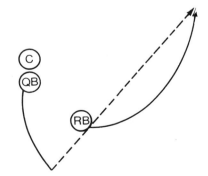

RUNNING BACK FLARE PASS

7 | Wide Receivers—Doing It Like the Pros

How to Choose a Wide Receiver

When a coach begins to look for a wide receiver he should go back to the faster boys who were timed in the forty-yard dash but were not strongly built to stand up under the rigors of the quarterback or running back position. Whether the boy is short or tall, if he "has wheels," then he's a natural for either a flanker position or a wide receiver position. For the purposes of this chapter, we will consider them as one and the same, though in certain offensive formations a flanker has to be able to block some pretty big people at the ends and must be big enough himself to have the horsepower to do the job. A flanker, in those tight formations like the *wing-T* and *slot* formations, may also be called on to run with the ball on inside reverses or delayed trap plays. Therefore, he is really a running back playing a flanker position.

If a coach likes to use both tight flanker–type formations and the wide-out sets, finding a player who can handle both roles will be more difficult. Instead of the relatively light-framed wide receiver, it becomes necessary to find a more muscular, heavier boy who can also run like the wind. Of course, as a last resort the coach may use two different boys, but that would begin to tell the defense what was going to happen. Without question, this is an important position on the team and the boys who play wide receiver rise to the occasion.

The fact that a youngster has a slight frame does not mean that he is without strength. Pass defenders will often try to intimidate the wide receiver whenever he runs downfield for a pass.

Obviously, the coach will look for the boys with the necessary qualities, but he will also look for players who have a great deal of pride and are willing to play a position that everyone can see. If a wide receiver drops a pass, he is usually out in the open, where his success or failure is exposed to all. Not all boys can handle this.

After the speed requirement is met, the coach will look for boys who can catch the ball. The size of the hands should be considered, along with the coordination with which the ball is caught. Sometimes a catch between a coach and a candidate is all that is necessary to determine if any talent is present. For those found acceptable, a passing drill with the quarterbacks throwing out patterns and some simple square-ins will provide another test for evaluation.

PHYSICAL REQUIREMENTS

The classical wide receiver is taller than average, slim but with well-developed muscles, and fast. It is uncommon to see boys of any height who are of heavy frame playing this speed-oriented position. Usually, the lighter the boy, the faster he can run; there are exceptions, however. Tall boys also have the advantage of being able to catch balls that may be thrown too high. They are also in a better position to catch a ball when they go up for a pass with a shorter defender.

This is not to say that shorter boys are not excellent material for wide receivers. On the contrary, their shorter stature often makes it possible for them to change direction better, which is of utmost importance in getting open to receive a pass. The ability to fake a defender into thinking you are going one way and then go another way is very vital to success in the passing game. Therefore, body control and coordinated footwork are also key physical requirements for a wide receiver.

Whether the boy is tall or short, he must develop his muscular structure to its limit. This will not only help increase his speed but will also make him more durable when he takes some of the hard shots that will come his way.

HOW TO CATCH THE BALL

Earlier we referred to a phrase that said a running back, in order to catch a pitch from the quarterback, "looks it" into his hands. This is

PASS-CATCHING RULE

the slogan of the wide receiver. His business is to catch the ball. If he touches it, he should catch it. Every time he catches a ball, anywhere and everywhere, he should look it into his hands. It must become an automatic reaction, almost an instinct.

In order to become expert at catching the ball, the wide receiver should first be shown that the ball is caught differently depending on where it is thrown. For example, a pass thrown above the wide receiver's head should be caught with the thumbs pointing inward and toward each other while the pinkies are extended outward (see diagram). A pass thrown below chest level should be caught with the thumbs pointing outward and the pinkies inward. When a ball is thrown to either side of the wide receiver, the thumbs-in position is used again. If you visualize your belt as the equator, anything above the equator to either side is thumbs in, but with the heels of the hands at the mouth of the opening of the grip and the thumbs at the back serving as the backstop to make sure the ball doesn't escape out the rear.

The fingers and hands must always be relaxed at the moment of impact. This technique prevents the ball from bouncing off and being dropped. Boys who do not use this technique to

The receiver has his hands poised with thumbs pointing in as the ball approaches him at shoulder height.

The receiver holds his fingers and hands relaxed as he surrounds the low throw and tucks it into his stomach.

With hands cupped and thumbs out, the receiver awaits the ball coming down to his belt.

The receiver pulls the ball into his body to avoid letting it bounce off his hands.

catch are said to have "brick hands" and can seldom be counted on to catch the ball. Even though the hands are relaxed (and not limp), they must react quickly upon contact to stop and seize the ball. Whenever possible, the ball should be caught with a pulling motion, as though you were pulling it in the same direction it was going in when you caught it. The pulling motion will help avoid the "brick hands" syndrome because, even with relaxed hands, if the ball is not pulled, it could still bounce off the wide receiver's hands. By learning to "look it" in as you pull it in one sweeping motion, the wide receiver will be doing it like the pros, and there is no better way.

At times you may have to dive for the ball and try to catch it any way you can. In these cases, all the basic rules are voided, except you should still try to follow the ball's flight until it hits your fingers. You may also have to catch it in your stomach or in your arms, but the best way for the long haul is to use your hands.

Another pitfall that a wide receiver should try to avoid is the habit of jumping up in the air to catch the ball. There will be times when you will have no choice but to leap for a pass thrown high in the air, but you should avoid jumping for those that are thrown at normal levels. Jumping makes it more difficult to catch the ball because you are shaking your body unnecessarily. You are also making yourself more vulnerable to injury if the defender should hit you while you're in midair. In addition, the play isn't over just because you caught the ball. Jumping will only serve to reduce your running speed and prevent you from gaining more yardage on the play.

Get into the habit of catching the ball, putting it into one arm or the other, and sprinting at least five to ten yards downfield after every pass you catch in practice. This, too, should become a reflex action and is all part of the pass play. Make it a routine action on every catch.

Footwork Requirements—Stance and Steps

The wide receiver has to have excellent agility to go along with his above-average speed. By learning to run well and under control, he will learn that almost every step he takes has a spe-

By jumping for a pass unnecessarily, the receiver often drops it because he jolted his body and jarred it loose.

cial importance. He must be graceful, nimble, and quick.

The wide receiver's stance is the same as that of the running back, discussed earlier. We don't believe in the upright stance that wide receivers are frequently permitted to use because we think that a quicker start can be made from a three-point stance. In the three-point stance the back foot should be slightly to the rear with its toes lined up with the laces of the front foot. With legs spread shoulder width apart, the wide receiver simply leans over and touches his right hand to the tips of the grass as his butt raises enough to lift the heel of the back foot.

His eyes should be turned toward the center and he should look for the ball to be snapped rather than simply rely on hearing the snap sound from the quarterback. Many times the crowd noise will be so loud that the quarterback will not be heard at all. Furthermore, if the wide receiver looks for the ball to move, he will be able to get off with the ball as quickly as possi-

The wide receiver's three-point stance should allow him to lean forward to provide a quick start downfield.

ble, a definite advantage for his penetration downfield to catch a pass.

The release off the line of scrimmage should be done at about the same speed on every pass route that a wide receiver runs. He should start off at about three-quarters speed, pumping his arms as he goes, with his eyes fixed straight ahead. There should be no tip-off to the defender as to where he is going or how fast he is going to run. That part of the route will come at a different time and place on the field, depending on the route being run.

How to Run the Pass Routes

There are nine different pass routes in our pass route tree (see diagram on page 60). Many of them start off looking the same, but at different distances downfield the wide receiver has to perform the route that was called for by the quarterback.

The 1 Route—The Sideline. Depending on the preferences of the coach, this route may be run three to ten yards deep. If the defender is playing loose—say, seven to ten yards off the line of scrimmage—a short out will be better. If he is playing tight, up to or close to the line of scrimmage, a deeper route will force him to run quickly with you. In addition, when you cut off your inside leg to turn out to the sideline, the quarterback will hit you while the defender is trying to recover from your quick change in direction.

The 2 Route—The Hook. This route can be run seven to eighteen yards deep and is designed to have the wide receiver turn on his full speed after five yards. When the defender tries to race with him, the wide receiver turns on his outside foot into the start of a post pattern and stops two steps later with his outside foot, hooks in, and comes back for the ball if it is not there waiting for him when he turns.

The 3 Route—The Sideline and Up. This becomes effective if the sideline has been used successfully during the course of a game. The left safety defending your right wide receiver may start to inch forward to attempt to pick off one of your quick out passes. The wide receiver should run his out, look at the quarterback for the ball as he nears the sideline, and then turn on his outside foot (the right foot, in this example) and race full speed up the sideline. Another wrinkle to this calls for the quarterback to fake

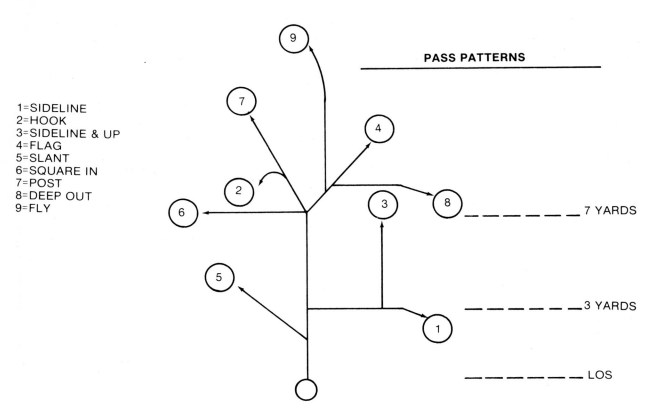

1=SIDELINE
2=HOOK
3=SIDELINE & UP
4=FLAG
5=SLANT
6=SQUARE IN
7=POST
8=DEEP OUT
9=FLY

PASS PATTERNS

7 YARDS

3 YARDS

LOS

SPLIT END–TIGHT END–FLANKER
PASS ROUTE TREE

throwing the ball when the wide receiver looks at him at the normal sideline point. This pump fake usually makes the defender come rushing up just as the wide receiver turns upfield and runs past him.

The 4 Route—The Flag. This is the opposite of the 7 Route, the *post*. The wide receiver, after his normal, slower five-yard start, goes full speed to about twelve to fifteen yards deep, hits his inside foot, throws his head inward as though he were running the post, and then heads for the flag at the corner of the goal line. The idea here is to force the defender to turn toward the post and force him to turn around to catch up with you as you head for the flag.

The 5 Route—The Slant. Different coaches run this in slightly different ways. Some start off straight (as in the diagram) and then cut in over the middle, while others head for the *slant* route as soon as the wide receiver comes off the line of scrimmage. We feel that by starting off straight,

the defender must take his first step backward and that little advantage may be all the wide receiver needs to get a split-second jump on him to get free. The cut is made on the outside foot about three to five yards downfield and should be made into an open slot between the outside safety/cornerback and the linebacker who will be retreating into his hook zone. This is called "finding an open seam" and will be covered in greater depth in chapter 9.

The 6 Route—The Square-in. This may be run from seven to fifteen yards deep, depending on your coach's preference or on the positioning of the linebackers and the deep safeties. The idea is to send a receiver across the middle of the field in between the short zone and the deep zone of the defense. A full-speed drive, stop, and cut off the outside foot are required of the wide receiver. As he runs across the field he should once again try to find the open seam for the quarterback to throw into.

The 7 Route—The Post. This route is the opposite of the *flag*; everything is the same except the wide receiver hits his outside foot, throws his head outside as though he were running the *flag*, then cuts in and looks for an open area. It is a more difficult route than the *flag* because the defender usually gets some help from another safety playing the deep middle. The wide receiver must be careful not to run into his area. This is not a problem when the deep safety is helping out on a double team on another wide receiver on the other side of the field.

The 8 Route—The Deep Out. This route is usually run from thirteen to eighteen yards deep after making the defender think that a *flag* or *fly* is being run. You should really be able to get him up to full speed when you hit your inside foot and cut as sharply as your body control will allow. Here again, be prepared to come back for the ball if it is not going to reach you because it is a long pass and there is plenty of time for the defender to recover and come back to make an interception.

The 9 Route—The Fly. As the name implies, you literally have to fly down the field for this to be effective. If a wide receiver has a recognized speed advantage over his coverage, this route should definitely be attempted. The key thing for the wide receiver to do is to try to get the defender to turn around. If you run the pattern right at him, he will be forced to turn and run with you. When he turns, you should turn the opposite way. This is sure to cause him to lose a step or two (see diagram at right).

OUTSMARTING THE DEFENSE

The best way for a wide receiver to outsmart the defenders is to run excellent pass routes. There must be solid teamwork between the quarterback and his receivers. If a wide receiver runs a given route one way on one play and then runs it a different way the next time, the quarterback won't know where to throw the ball and either will be sacked or will throw an interception.

In practice, when there are no defenders, the wide receiver will tend to run the routes to the

depth that the coach has specified and the quarterback will have little difficulty knowing when and where to throw. But, in a game, with defenders in many different defenses ranging from man to man to zone and to a combination of both, unless the quarterback has a good idea of what the wide receiver is going to do, he will definitely be at a disadvantage.

The solution is to communicate. The coach, the quarterback, and the wide receiver must get together and decide how the routes should be adjusted to cope with the defense against which they are playing. The depth of the cuts may have to be changed; the *hook-in* may have to be

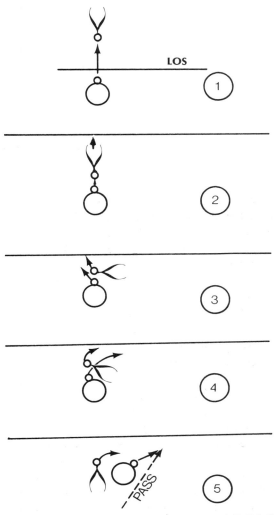

TURNING A PASS DEFENDER AROUND

changed to a *hook-out*; the *post* might be run more like a semi–*square-in*, and so on.

There is also an opportunity to improvise. This means to make up a special pattern that will exploit a weakness in the defense for which you have no route to use. The wide receiver should also keep in mind that he may have to scramble after he has run his route, only to find the quarterback running for his life under pass rush pressure from the big defensive front. In this situation, the wide receiver should run into an open seam and stop, hoping that the quarterback will see him and have enough time to throw it to him. While stopped, he should continue to look around to make sure that someone isn't sneaking up on him for an interception.

Above all else, make your fakes and cuts as quickly and sharply as you can. The best way to get open is to change direction sharply, to make your defender think you're going one way and then to change direction and go another way. If you do this often enough, and you can run and catch the ball, you'll be a great weapon for scoring.

TRAINING TO DEVELOP SKILLS

Speed, moves, and sure hands are the primary skills that a wide receiver must have to be good. We discussed the techniques to be used to increase your speed in chapter 7, on running backs. You have to build up your thigh muscles and all your other leg muscles to enable you to pick up and lower your legs as fast as you can. Running sprints over a long period of time will help you do this. A wide receiver who must also learn to vary his speed at different places on the field on different pass routes should run two kinds of sprints. One should be the full-out type of sprint in which he starts from his regular stance and runs as hard as he can from start to finish. The other requires him to run five to ten yards at three-quarters speed and then shift into

high gear for his full speed. Both of these must be run frequently to gain the most improvement.

Moves can be practiced best against an opponent. A good technique is for two wide receivers to practice with each other. While one plays offense, the other plays defense. This will allow each to help the other by pointing out things that were done well and things that needed improvement. The defender can say that he was either fooled or not fooled by a move. And, if the wide receiver gets open, he can assume that at least he was able to outmaneuver his defender. Try to have a coach observe you to get his expert criticism.

Remember that moves require body control and simple, quick reactions. Don't clutter them up with dragging feet at the turn or fancy hip wiggles and arm waves. Just get from where you are to where you want to be smoothly and with balance.

To improve your hands, you have to catch and catch and catch. Have a catch with anyone and be sure the ball is thrown to all sides of you, low and high, and hard and soft. Have your partner throw wobbly passes and end-over-end passes to test your ability to handle these balls, look them in, and put them away.

A really good drill is to have a wide receiver stand with his back to the person throwing the ball to him. When the ball is on its way, from a distance of about ten to fifteen yards, the passer says, "Turn." The wide receiver has to spin around quickly, locate the ball, get his hands into position, look it in, and put it away in a split second. This helps these actions become automatic to the wide receiver.

Of course, the best practice is to run pass routes with your quarterback throwing to you. You must get the feel of his ball and you must develop the timing that is so important to a good quarterback/wide receiver combination. Practice as often as you can, with or without the team. You will never get too much of it.

8 | Tight Ends—Blocking and Catching

HOW TO CHOOSE A TIGHT END

Tight ends must be big people because they have to block big people who play defensive tackle and defensive end. If they had no pass receiving responsibility, they would have to come from the same pool of players as offensive and defensive tackles. However, because of the importance of the tight end in the passing offense, the coach must now try to seek out some big people who can also run with good speed and catch the football. These are qualities that are often hard to find in high school and at lower levels.

PHYSICAL REQUIREMENTS

When college coaches go out to recruit tight ends, they benefit from the screening process already conducted in high school by the coaches at that level, who have spent a good deal of time finding and developing tight ends. The difficulty is that many players who grow to be 6' 3" or taller don't develop their coordination until they are older as compared to boys who are average height or shorter. Therefore, recruiting a tight end for a college team can be tricky because many boys who were forced to play tackle in high school because they couldn't catch and run suddenly blossom into outstanding tight ends in college. On the other side of the coin, boys who were big enough to play tight end in high school, usually 6' to 6' 2", get to college only to find that they are too small. Since many college coaches are switching to a multiple, wide-out offense, the position is in greater and greater demand. Therefore, any youngster in high school who has the appro-

A big tight end shows his soft hands as he pulls the pass in for a touchdown, all alone in the end zone.

TIGHT END BLOCK ON DEFENSIVE END AT THE CORNER

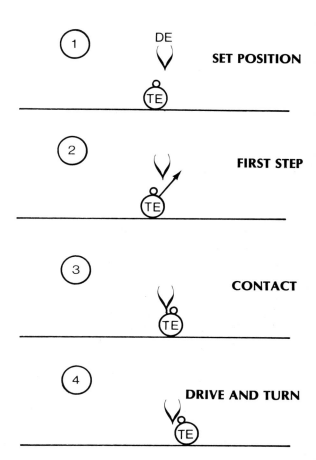

priate size and talent will discover that he is much sought after by college scouts.

In terms of stature, the tight end should be as big as anyone on the team. His agility and speed should set him apart from other big men, and his overall coordination should be evident in the way he runs and catches. His muscular development should be equal to the other big men because he has just as many strength requirements as they have. In particular, his upper body strength is important in order to block effectively and to force his way free when an opposing linebacker tries to keep him from releasing for a pass.

Tight End Blocking Responsibilities

In most tight end formations, the tight end will be blocking on a defensive tackle or a defensive end. The direction from their defensive coach will usually be to play on the outside shoulder of the tight end in order to prevent him from blocking them in or down to permit a run around that end. And, as you might suspect, the tight end's offensive coach is telling him to do

just that on any play that is headed outside or, as it is termed in football, "around the corner."

This is a very difficult block to throw because the defender's strength and momentum have to be overcome or at least neutralized in order to give the running back time to get past that area (see diagram above). The most common block to be thrown in this situation is the shoulder block, which requires the tight end to beat the defender off the ball, get his inside shoulder into him, and get his head and neck under the defender's outside shoulder. After that, it is a matter of leg drive, with the tight end always trying to turn the defender's body away from the hole and using the head and neck muscles to apply additional presure to help turn him.

Another frequent blocking situation calls for the tight end to release through the line of

TIGHT END SEAL BLOCK ON LINEBACKER

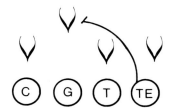

TIGHT END DOUBLE TEAM BLOCK

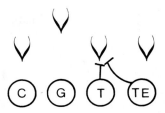

scrimmage and come down on the nearest line-backer to seal him off and put a big obstacle in the pursuit lane that frequently uses the area just past the line of scrimmage to chase a running back going around end. This block can be either a shoulder block or a cross body block, depending on the position of the linebacker. If the tight end can get close to him, the shoulder block should be used. If the linebacker is running away from the tight end, then his best bet is to throw the cross body because it gives him more blocking surface and will probably allow him to get a piece of the linebacker (see diagram above left).

In order to open a running hole, many coaches ask the tight end to throw a double team block on the big defensive tackle who may be playing opposite the offensive tackle (see diagram above right). In this situation, the offensive tackle will drive his right shoulder up and through the defensive tackle's chest while he forces his head under the defensive tackle's right arm. This will often stop the defensive tackle's forward thrust; then, when the tight end applies his strength, the defensive tackle gets blown out of the hole area. The tight end's job is to come down the line of scrimmage on a diagonal angle to get his left shoulder into the defensive tackle's chest as he raises his forearms to apply pressure on both sides of his shoulder. The leg drive and head and neck turn will drive the defensive tackle back to give the running back the room he needs to go outside the double team area and run to daylight. These and other blocks will be covered in depth in chapter 10, on blocking.

How to Run the Pass Routes

The pass routes that were reviewed in chapter 7 generally apply to the tight end as well. There are some variations, however, because the tight end is usually in a crowd and is always closer to the middle of the field. In addition, his release problem is often more difficult.

The wide receiver often has the advantage of knowing where his defender is because he is usually right out there in front of him. The tight end may have this insight, too, but more often he may be covered by a variety of people or by no one in a zone defense. It is important to any receiver to know whether he is up against man-to-man coverage, zone coverage, or a combination.

It is for this reason that many coaches run a *square-in* pattern early in the game to see whether a defender follows the receiver across the field or releases him into the adjoining zone. On every pass route that a tight end runs, he should be aware of the coverage because it will greatly influence how he runs his patterns. For example, if he is against man-to-man coverage, when he runs his *square-in* his concern should be for a good fake and sharp cut to get away from his man. The coach may want to set up a pass play that empties the adjoining zone to allow the tight end to get free of his man and be open for the reception (see diagram at top of page 66). On the other hand, if the coverage is zone, the pass play would be the same but the tight end would run his route differently to get open in the seam between the zones for the

PRO-RIGHT–TIGHT END SQUARE-IN
VS MAN COVERAGE

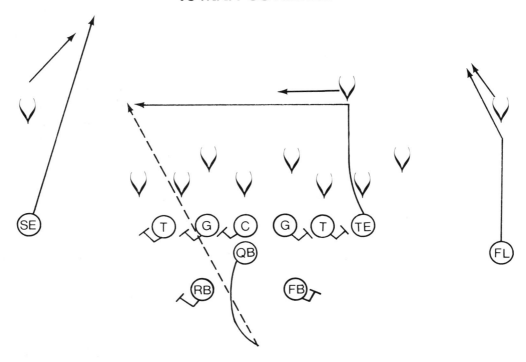

PRO-RIGHT–TIGHT END SQUARE-IN
VS ZONE COVERAGE

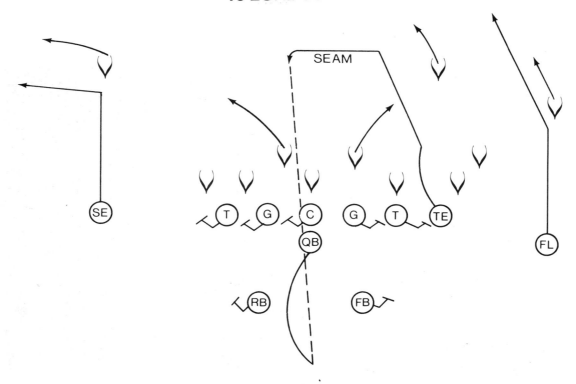

reception (see diagram at bottom of page 66). The release problem occurs when a linebacker, knowing that a pass play is anticipated, stands over the tight end's three-point stance and tries to prevent him from releasing downfield to run his pass route. The tight end's stance is exactly like any other offensive lineman's stance (see chapter 9) because he is more often forced to contend with the linebacker pressure on him.

There are two basic ways to contend with the linebacker jamming technique. One is to take a very short step with your front foot, then push off it and either spin away from the linebacker or use your forearm to push him off you as you drive your legs past him. The other technique is to release on a slant, either toward the middle of the field or to the outside of the field, depending on what kind of a pass route you are running. If it is an out pattern, release to the outside and push off with your forearm as you go. If it is an inside route, go immediately in that direction as you come out of your starting stance and forearm your way past him. Remember, he's not allowed to hold you or your jersey. If he does this often, on your way back to the huddle ask the nearest official to have one of their crew watch for it on subsequent plays.

OUTTHINKING THE DEFENDERS

Because the tight end is a blocker as well as a pass receiver, he is a vital member of the offense for the defense to keep an eye on. Most defensive coaches will tell their strong safety (the defender who normally covers the tight end on man-to-man coverage) to key on the tight end to learn what kind of play the offense is running. The word *key* means that, based on what the tight end does, the defense will have a key to the secret and be able to react accordingly when the offensive play begins. The thing they normally look for is whether the tight end blocks someone on the line of scrimmage or releases downfield for a pass. The reasoning is partially sound. If the tight end blocks, then the safety can disregard him as a pass receiver, at least for the moment, and can come rushing up to the line of scrimmage as he reads the backfield action to help make the tackle. If the tight end releases, the safety now has to freeze for a moment to see what's happening before he reacts.

The difficulty with the key analysis is that if the tight end releases on a slant over the middle, he may be trying to get downfield for a block because the ball is being run in that direction or

The tight end's stance must allow him to throw a block or to release downfield for a pass.

Taking an inside release, the tight end slants over the middle and looks for the ball coming over the crowd.

he may be running a pass pattern in that direction. And, if the tight end blocks, he may be blocking for only a second or two to make the safety think it is a running play; then he will try to sneak out into the flat or over the middle for a delayed pass from the quarterback.

The tight end must also try to disguise the fact that he is going to block down on a linebacker. The best way to do this is to look straight ahead at all times so that no one can read your eyes to get an idea of the direction in which you plan to go. Some tight ends make the mistake of only looking at a linebacker when they are going to block him. Try to conceal everything you do. Keep a blank look on your face and execute exactly as your coach directs you because someone is watching you on every play.

TRAINING TO DEVELOP SKILLS

The tight ends must do everything that the wide receivers were asked to do in their training review (see chapter 7). They must improve their running speed and their ability to fake defenders in order to get free on pass patterns, and they need hands that can catch the ball with all the skill of a wide receiver. Their strength requirements are driven by two needs that a wide receiver seldom has to face. The most important is the blocking talent necessary to move and stop the big defensive tackles and defensive ends; the other is to get away from the linebacker who is trying to prevent the tight end from releasing on a pass play.

In order to develop this strength, the tight end needs to develop his upper body and leg mus-

One tight end shows perfect pass-catching form as the ball arrives while another tight end observes.

The tight end gets free against man-to-man coverage on a square-in pattern and reaches up to make the reception.

cles. Both can be achieved through a weights program, especially with a weights bench and/or with a universal body-building machine that most high schools now have. The tight end cannot go as far with his strength buildup as a defensive tackle or offensive tackle because it may tend to make him less flexible for the raising and movement of his arms for pass receiving, but the strength targets should be just a little bit lower. As for his leg development, running sprints is just as important to his speed as it is to the wide receiver.

Blocking skills can be developed best under the coach's direction in conjunction with other players of comparable size. Blocking techniques and stances will be reviewed in chapter 10. Once the basics are known and understood, you need nothing more than frequent practice in order to sharpen your skills. Get a teammate of about your size, hopefully another tight end, put on your helmets and shoulder pads, and practice one-on-one as often as you can. Blocking is a skill that can and must be developed if you are to help your team.

9 | Offensive Linemen—Infantry on the March

How to Choose Offensive Interior Linemen

Every team has its unsung heroes—the players who do the work that must be done if the team is going to be successful, but who never get the recognition they often deserve. This is the situation that usually faces the boys that play the offensive interior linemen positions. Everyone knows they are vital to the team's success, but hardly anyone other than their parents and their coaches know who they are.

Finding boys who have the physical as well as mental requirements for these positions is not an easy task for a coach. This is particularly true of the mental criteria. Many young boys are driven by personalities that require them to be heard as well as seen and couldn't tolerate the obscurity of being a center, guard, or tackle. However, there are other boys who get full satisfaction out of knowing that they are helping their team and that they are playing a position as difficult as any on the field.

Physical Requirements

Centers and tackles have about the same overall size and physical requirements. Of the two, the boys who are quicker and more alert mentally should be tried at center. This is because their blocking assignments and difficulties can use quickness and because the center has to be tuned in to what the quarterback is doing with snap sounds and audibles and needs alertness or the team will suffer considerably.

Most teams will put a big man defensively at nose guard to play opposite the center in an odd-man front and will instruct him to try to punish him physically to soften him up. The nose guard will also try to slant to either side of

The center takes his proper stance and alertly awaits to snap the ball when the quarterback calls the snap sound.

the center and will be involved with a number of stunts with one or both middle linebackers. All of this means trouble for a center if he is not quick, big, and strong—as big and as strong as anyone on offense.

The offensive tackles should be the slower of the boys trying out for interior offensive linemen positions; if all other things are equal, they should also be the bigger boys. This is necessary because most defenses put their biggest, toughest players at defensive tackle and they are the guys the offensive tackles have to contend with all game long. The offensive guards are usually the shorter of the big players because, along with their shorter stature, they often have greater quickness, running speed, and agility. These qualities are vital to this position because guards are called on to pull out of the line and lead the blocking around end on end sweeps. They are also asked to pull and trap defensive tackles or defensive ends and are often required

to pull back on pass blocking when they are uncovered by a defensive lineman.

All of the interior linemen must build up their bodies, muscles, and strength to handle the vigorous blocking tasks with which they are faced. They must also understand the offensive approach to every game and be prepared to adjust as the defensive alignments make it necessary. A great deal of intelligence is required to play these positions as well as they must be played, particularly as defenses get more complex.

BUILDING YOUR STRENGTH FOR THE JOB

As we have stated on a few occasions thus far, any player who requires great strength to execute the requirements of his position must take it upon himself to make the most of his body. It is amazing to see the progress that some boys make when they start on a weights program and

The center fires out at the nose guard at the instant the ball was snapped to the quarterback to start the play.

dedicate themselves to continuing it until they reach their objectives.

Universal gyms have made it possible to build up any muscle in your body if you follow the guidelines that have been established for their use. It would not be wise to try to advise any boy on what he should do with this type of equipment or any other weight and strength developing equipment without knowing the boy's height, weight, body structure, and muscle development. It is sufficient simply to point out that because each of you is different to begin with, what you can eventually develop into is not possible to predict.

Rather, it is far better to talk to your physical education teacher, coach, or a representative or salesman of weight training equipment to get specific advice after that person has seen and evaluated your physique. There should be no doubt in your mind that it is both right and necessary to approach this problem in this manner because it is possible to do yourself some harm if the proper techniques and goals are not followed. Once you have a clear path to follow, it is up to you to give your time and energy to make the most out of your bodybuilding program. It will be hard work that pays off.

AGILITY AND QUICKNESS

These are two terms that you will hear for as long as you play football, and they are as important as any other aspect of your preparedness. In fact, there are many coaches who believe that the biggest improvement in football over the last fifty years has been brought about by the advances that have been made in the agility and quickness of the big men of the game.

When you watch college and NFL football on TV, you often see a very big defensive lineman catching up to or running down a running back from behind. Sometimes it is difficult to believe what you are seeing, but it happens so often now that it is not considered as amazing as it once was. Agility and quickness made it possible, and it all began back when the players were boys and they were put through a number of drills to sharpen their skills and abilities in this area. The section on practice (chapter 17) highlights a variety of things to do to improve your skill. To a coach agility means the ability to react quickly with your hands, arms, legs, and feet. Everything you do on a football field is done better if you do it quickly. Therefore, when you are nimble and light on your feet, even though you are as big as anyone else on the field, you do not have to sacrifice speed for size. When you learn the drills to use, perform them often and with great concentration to get the most out of them. The last thing you want to find out is that you can do all the things the boy ahead of you on the depth chart can do, except he does them more quickly and with quicker reflexes.

STANCE, THRUST, AND FOLLOW-THROUGH

Once you have developed your body to the level required to play your position, you have to work on your technique in order to execute the assignments that your position requires. It is not possible to perform with any level of competence unless you start from the stance suited to your height and weight and can launch your body and maintain the advantage that your start should have given you.

The stance requirements for players vary with their body size and structure. The basic ap-

The offensive linemen's stance must be low, balanced, and ready to thrust at a defender in all directions.

proach is to take a standing position with your feet shoulder width apart. This means that if you were to hang a weight from a string off the tip of your shoulder, the weight would rub along the outer edge of your shoe. This is necessary for proper balance of your weight and to ensure quick movement of your feet, both straight ahead and laterally.

Your left heel should be parallel with the toe of your right foot in order to hold your weight on the balls of both feet. As you squat, your right hand should extend directly downward from your right shoulder and your left forearm should rest on the inside of your left thigh. You should squat only as low as you need to to make your back parallel to the ground. Your butt should be raised to make your back parallel and to get your right foot up on its ball with the front of that foot dug into the playing surface for leverage. This leverage is vital to your ability to thrust forward at the snap of the ball to provide the fire power that many blocks require in order to be successful. (The details on each block and its execution will follow in chapter 10.)

When you are settled into this three-point stance, be careful not to put too much weight on the front hand and fingers or it will be very difficult to pull away from this stance and pull

out for a sweep or a trap. It will also make pass blocking drop-back more difficult. Some players make the mistake of leaning farther forward when they are going forward and of leaning backward off their front hand when they are going backward or sideways. Pressure on the front hand is easy for an opponent to see. Therefore, you may be tipping off what the play is—a run or perhaps a pass—when your knuckles get white from bearing up under your body weight.

The biggest advantage an offensive lineman has over his opponent on the line of scrimmage is that he knows when the ball will be snapped for the start of each play. The defender has to wait to see the ball move before he can start his charge across the line of scrimmage. Therefore, if you are to make the most of the momentum your body weight will provide as you throw your block, you must be prepared to launch your body quickly after the snap sound is made. This is made possible when you have a good stance with your back foot ready for push-off and you anticipate the shouting of the snap sound by the quarterback. All of this is called "getting off the mark." It is as important to the offensive lineman as it is to the track man who is trying to win a sixty-yard dash.

When you have learned how to launch your body with all the quickness you can deliver, the

The offensive line is ready to fire out on the snap sound to get the advantage of momentum when they hit.

next effort that is required is to follow through with your power and sustain the advantage you have established over your opponent. Blocking effectiveness is far more than the original thrust across the line of scrimmage. Defensive linemen are strong and, because they can use their hands, they can turn your initial advantage in their favor unless you follow through. By definition, this means that you need to take a second and a third step, and even more in some cases, as you drive your legs to push your upper body into and through the defender. In fact, you should continue to throw your block until the whistle blows to make certain that you have done your job from start to finish.

Quick hitting plays often require a block that lasts for a few seconds, but there are many delayed plays like draws and traps in addition to pass plays that require a long, sustained block to ensure success. Probably the biggest and most

The blockers get off the mark and into their blocks as the quarterback opens up to his left to hand off the ball.

The offensive guard and tackle start from their stances and deliver their blocks quickly to move the defenders.

frequent mistake made by offensive linemen is to give up on their block too soon and allow the defender to make the tackle.

OUTSMARTING YOUR OPPONENTS

An offensive lineman can do a number of things to gain an advantage over his counterpart across the line of scrimmage. The most beneficial one is to vary your blocking technique so as to confuse your opponent. If you constantly throw a shoulder block, it won't be long before he finds the best way to ward off your attack and stops running plays in your area. Once you have mastered all the blocking techniques your coach wants you to use, try to mix them up in your handling of your opponent. If he doesn't know how you are coming at him, it will make it far more difficult for him to cope with you.

At the same time you are trying to confuse him, he will be trying to mix up his attack to make it more difficult for you to get him. Try to learn what his tendencies are. For example, on obvious pass plays, does he always try to go around your outside? If so, inform the quarterback, and maybe a draw play will gain good yardage through your inside. Any indication you can get about what he is likely to do can be a big benefit for your team. The average player doesn't know how important the interior lineman can be in the development of strategy during the course of the game. Another very important part of the struggle "in the pit" is the comparative toughness of the combatants. Is your opponent unable to stand the physical strain and abuse to which he is being subjected? Try to read his reaction when you and your teammate blast him with a double team block. In effect, you should be looking for someone who shows that pain is getting to him. When you find an opponent like this, tell your coach and quarterback and run some more overwhelming plays at him to soften him even more. If you can accomplish this, you will soon "own him," as the football vernacular goes, and the yardage that is gained through your hole will be important to the success of the team. When the game is over, you will know how much you have contributed to the win.

TRAINING TO DEVELOP SKILLS

The primary skills of the offensive linemen are strength, agility, quickness, and blocking technique. We have already reviewed the roll of strength and stressed the importance of developing agility through the use of drills. But a few other things can be done to get your bodies ready for a season and to keep it ready during the season. One of these is a running program and the other is designed to improve your agility through coordination.

Running is important to any athlete, but it has a particularly valuable benefit to the endurance of big athletes. Whereas the running backs and wide receivers were made aware of the value of running sprints to increase their speed, linemen should embark on a distance running program to increase their stamina. Stamina is another word for staying power. If you are able to produce an effort for only part of a game, the remainder of the game will find you unable to help your team.

Linemen face a strength requirement on almost every play of a game. By the time the second half arrives, those who have not properly conditioned themselves will begin to weaken and will fail to open holes or protect the quarterback on pass plays. Distance running has long been accepted by coaches as one of the best ways to build stamina.

In preseason, begin by running a half mile on a school track, if possible, or over a measured route. Do not run in the heat of the day during hot summer months or you may become dehydrated and weak. Any dizziness that you may incur should be discussed with your doctor. It is wise to point out that any extended physical effort or training program should not begin until you have had a physical examination and a doctor's approval. Let him know what you intend to do and get and heed any advice he may wish to give you.

After running a half mile for five days, increase the distance by a half mile on every successive week until you get to three miles. This goal will mean that you have been running for six weeks and have begun to develop the staying power necessary to increase your stamina. Maintain this level until the team's official practices begin and then switch to the training program that your coach establishes for you.

It is also important to run some sprints to increase your speed. The best way to do that is to sprint the last forty yards of every half mile and then coast the next forty yards until you can reestablish the rhythm of your regular pace. When the season begins the coach will provide for sprints in his training program. The best coordination developer for big linemen is to learn how to jump rope and to increase the speed with which you turn the rope. There are some excellent jump ropes on the market with handles that make it possible to accelerate the speed of the rope as you jump. Begin slowly and concentrate on jumping without missing before you try to increase the speed. This exercise can be done before and during the season but must be done under the right conditions to be effective. Use sneakers and try to jump on either concrete or a bare wooden floor. Also remember that jumping rope is intended to improve your rhythm and timing to enable you to use your legs and feet in coordination with your arms and body. Try to develop a rhythmic beat as you get your entire body higher and higher off the floor. When you have become more skilled at it, you may be able to alternate feet, landing on one foot and then the other. There hasn't been a football player who has not improved his footwork and agility after learning to jump rope with ease and skill.

Blocking techniques and training programs used to develop them will be covered in the following chapter. As indicated in the review in chapter 8, they are best developed under the coach's guidance. Blocking is a skill that you can't get along without because it is the tool of your trade. After having learned the various techniques as your coach wants them performed, you will have to seek every opportunity to practice them with someone of your own size. This skill is one of the two basics of football that must be learned and done well. The other is tackling. As is true in military tactics, without the infantry the army can't march. So it is in football: without the interior offensive linemen the ball can't be moved on the ground. Without a doubt this is where the war is won, in the army and in football.

10 | Blocking Skills and Techniques

Football is a game that brings out many of the natural talents of an athlete, perhaps because it is a combination of running and throwing the ball or because of the enthusiasm involved in tackling and overwhelming an opponent who is trying to score against your team. The one vital skill that doesn't seem to come naturally is that of blocking; yet, those teams that learn to do it well have a much greater chance of success.

It is a wise coach who applies a good deal of his team's time to practice blocking. And it is a wise young athlete who takes the time to learn to block well because it is a rare talent and one that can make football an extremely satisfying game to play. At one time or another, every offensive player may be called on to throw a block. Because there are many different situations in which a block is needed, there are many different blocking techniques that must be used.

OFFENSIVE BLOCKING MADE EASY

The most successful blockers are those who find a variety of ways to get an advantage over an opponent. Once the advantage has been gained, a sound execution of a blocking technique must be applied. We will take a look at how to gain advantages, which technique to apply, and how, in each situation.

For many years football coaches directed their linemen to move specific defenders in certain directions in order to open the hole through which the play was designed to go. And, if it happened that a defender was in that hole and could not be turned in the direction the coach wanted, the play was doomed to failure. There was no flexibility in either the blocking rules or the directions the back could run.

As coaches became more aware of changes

All the blockers on the offensive line show excellent form as they wait for the execution of the play.

that were necessary to achieve success, a new philosophy developed and a new rule for blocking was established. It became known as the "soft" blocking rule and permitted the blocker greater latitude in execution of his block. It gave the blocker the option to get his man out of the way in any way he could and meant that the running back would alter his direction based on what the blocker was able to do in the vicinity of the hole. In other words, though the play was designed to hit a certain spot on the line of scrimmage, the running back was to head in that direction after getting the ball, but he had to be prepared to veer off into any open slot that his blockers were able to create for him. The running back was told to "run to daylight" and to "hit the seam," and many other coined phrases were used to advise him to keep his eyes open and run through any opening he could

find. The era of the running back lowering his head and simply driving through a mass of bodies was over—unless, of course, there was no daylight and he had no choice other than to make the most of the situation.

The blocker was also directed to use any one of many different blocking techniques that he felt were best suited to get his man out of the play. To give him this additional flexibility, many new blocking techniques were developed and practiced very frequently. Fifty years ago only a few blocking styles were taught and used. The most common were the double team, the shoulder, the crab, and the cross body blocks. Offensive and defensive lines were jammed in close together to minimize splits between players. The double team blocks were simply a matter of brute strength; holes were seldom opened; and the backs dove into or over the pile of linemen.

The second most significant change that occurred to help the blocking problem was the use of line splits between offensive linemen. A line split is the distance between the center and the guard, the guard and the tackle, and the tackle and the end (see diagram below left). As you can readily see, the area that is covered in an old alignment is considerably narrower than a typical new alignment often used by coaches at all levels today. The fear of using line splits was that defenders could find gaps in the offensive front through which they could stunt and blitz and that defensive linemen could slant or loop around the offensive linemen and get into your backfield. There is a sound basis for those fears—those things do happen. However, it is also sound strategy to find a way to open up the distance between defensive linemen to help create the daylight through which your backs can run. Unfortunately, you can't do the latter without doing the former (see diagram below).

TIGHT END SPLITS—OLD ALIGNMENT

YARDS BETWEEN

WIDE LINE SPLITS—NEW ALIGNMENT

YARDS BETWEEN

WIDE LINE SPLITS—WITHOUT DEFENSIVE ADJUSTMENT

WIDE LINE SPLITS—WITH DEFENSIVE ADJUSTMENT

If the defensive line doesn't spread the players to match your players, then you have the advantage of running around them because your linemen would have excellent down-blocking angles on them and down blocks are the easiest blocks to throw (see diagram above). The use of line splits varies slightly, depending on the type of play being used. Some general rules are that you tighten up your splits on passes and outside plays; you open them on all inside plays. Field goal and extra point teams must close their gaps tightly, but some coaches punt with wide splits while others use no splits at all. In addition, all offensive linemen are instructed to use their own discretion regarding line splits until they find the best advantage they can get in dealing with their opponent. For example, if you are the left tackle and an end sweep is being run around

The defensive linemen can be seen in the gaps between the wide splits in the offensive line.

The offensive line takes tight splits as the wide receiver goes into motion for the start of a pass play.

After getting a down block advantage from their line splits, offensive linemen lead the running back around right end.

LEFT TACKLE—NORMAL SPLIT

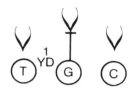

LEFT TACKLE—EXTRAWIDE SPLIT WITH DEFENSIVE ADJUSTMENT

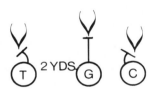

LEFT TACKLE—EXTRAWIDE SPLIT WITHOUT DEFENSIVE ADJUSTMENT

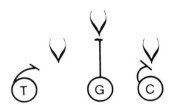

right end, there is no precise line split that you have to take that will guarantee the play's success. Where you line up has very little bearing on the play. At a time like this, you should take an extra wide split to your left away from the left guard, just to see what the defensive tackle opposite you does in reaction to your move (see diagram above left).

If the defensive tackle moves out with you, the quarterback should be given that data and perhaps the next play will be run between you and the left guard because there will be a much wider gap between the defensive tackle and the nose guard. If you can block the linebacker, there may be some big yardage to be gained. On the other hand, if the defensive tackle does not move out with you, there is a down-block advantage to be had and the quarterback may want to run outside you on the next play (see diagram above right).

Making minor adjustments with your line splits is an experiment that you should do throughout a ball game. It should help you determine which of your actions give you the best advantages to help you find running room for your backs. These little things are hardly seen or noticed, and you should try to do them a few inches at a time to avoid allowing your defender to know that you are trying to set him up for a kill. Be sure to mix up what you are doing to avoid any pattern. If you tighten your splits very noticeably on pass plays, the defense will soon get a tip-off as to when your team is throwing the ball. Once again, when the distance of your split doesn't really make a difference in the play, tighten up to the same distance that you do on pass plays to confuse your defender. The whole situation is like a game of chess—moves and counter moves. You should have the advantage because you know where the ball is going, and you should be able to find the best advantage you can get.

HOW TO EXECUTE VARIOUS BLOCKS FOR THE RUN

After the coach has reviewed your stance and thrust technique and put you through frequent blocking sled and dummies drills, you are ready to learn to block live against your teammates. Depending on the level of ball, the coach may want to use all or some of the following blocking styles, or he may have variations of them that he prefers. His direction is the final word on what you do and how you do it, but the following are some basic techniques that will be good for you to know.

SHOULDER FIRE BLOCK

This is the basic shoulder block that begins when you fire off with your back foot taking the first step as you dig the ball of your front foot into the turf to provide the thrust. Drive your shoulder into the numbers of your opponent and thrust your head to the hole side, driving with short, choppy steps. Keep your back arched to allow your butt to drive your shoulders on through your man to overcome his strength with your momentum.

The left side of the offensive line throw shoulder fire blocks to drive open a hole for the running back.

The center uses a reverse shoulder block to move the nose guard away from the flow of the play.

REVERSE SHOULDER BLOCK

When an opponent is in your inside gap and you have to prevent his penetration and take him out of the play, this is the block to use. Take your first step with your near foot (the one closest to the defender) down the line of scrimmage. Then lower and drive your outside shoulder (the one farthest away from him) into the break of his leg above his knee as you drive your head into his crotch area. Follow through by driving with short, choppy steps and then roll into him to take him off his feet.

NEAR SHOULDER BLOCK

When your opponent is on your inside shoulder or outside shoulder, take your first step

The on-side guard (number 68) throws a near shoulder block as the off-side guard pulls to trap the defensive end.

with your nearest foot toward his crotch, with your toes pointing straight upfield. Stay low and drive your near shoulder into the break of his farthest leg as your head comes up through his crotch. Follow through as above with short, choppy steps and a roll to take him down.

REACH SHOULDER BLOCK

Reach blocks are used when you want to block a man on your outside to your inside. You may also use the reach block for someone on your head (heads up) and on your inside or outside shoulder but never when the attack is coming directly through your hole. It will prevent penetration but is difficult to move a man out of the hole. Pivot on your far foot and step with your near foot (pivot and step) as you fire your head past the defender's outside knee. Thrust your inside shoulder into that knee and regain a squared position to the goal line and drive.

The on-side guard (number 60) throws a reach shoulder block as his teammate blocks out on the defensive end.

REACH CRAB BLOCK

This block may be used when the defender is playing in the same places as in the reach shoulder block. Drive your head and inside elbow past the defender's outside knee; at the same time bring your inside leg into a crabbing position outside the inside leg. Your initial pivot and step should have brought your body across his and both of his legs should be inside, against your torso. With your arms crawling on the ground on his outside and your inside leg crabbing on the inside, your other leg must try to turn your body until you are square to the line of scrimmage. By scrambling with arms and legs churning, you will prevent his penetration into your backfield.

DOUBLE TEAM (POST AND LEAD) BLOCK

The post man in the double team is the man who prevents the penetration, and the lead man is the man who turns the opponent away from the hole. The post must explode into the defender with the shoulder closest to the lead man, taking his first step with the foot on the same side. As the shoulder comes up through the numbers, the head must be slipped to the inside hip if the man is sliding off to the side away from the lead man. Attempt to drive the man up and straight back. The lead man takes his first step with his near foot toward the defender's crotch and drives his near shoulder into the break of the nearest knee. With both arms raised, elbows extending parallel to their shoulders to broaden his blocking surface, the lead man must drive his head up into the outer rib cage of the defender, square off his butt with the post man, and drive the opponent up and back. It is vital that both of the blockers stay close together and that their bodies are square to the line of scrimmage to prevent the defender from slipping off one man so he only has to deal with the other. This block is the best way to guarantee a hole and is often used on opponents that one man can't handle.

CROSS BLOCK

This block may be used by any adjoining pair of offensive linemen who are constantly or frequently faced with opponents who are heads up on them. It is a good way to get an advantage by setting up a good blocking angle. The man who goes first should be the one dealing with the quickest defender. His block should be either a driving near shoulder technique or a reverse shoulder technique (see both above). His angle of attack will provide momentum to drive the man away from the hole. The second man must use the pivot and trap technique, which is covered below. The cross block is excellent to open a hole between two side-by-side opponents who often don't have a linebacker playing between them. Once the running back gets through the hole, he may spring free into the secondary.

TRAP BLOCK

In order to pull out quickly to throw a trap block, it is necessary to pivot on the far foot from the direction in which you are going and then take a short step with the other foot on a 45-degree angle away from the line of scrimmage. This angle away from the line is necessary to avoid making contact with any other lineman, either offensive or defensive. As the first step is being taken, the lead arm should be pulling the body around while the other arm and hand swing low (as though some grass were being pulled) to keep the body balanced. The contact with the defender must be an explosion up and through him, driven by the thrust of the stepping foot. The block must be aimed at his inside hip to ensure hitting him at the center of his body where the strength of the block will do the most good.

INFLUENCE BLOCK

This is a fake block that is intended to make the defender think you are going to block him, but you are really setting him up for someone else to block. By taking a short jab step with the inside foot, you cause the defender to freeze for a moment as he anticipates what you intend to do with him. As the jab step is taken, pivot on it, pull your arms around to turn your body, and block the first man to your outside. Usually, by the time the influence blocker moves out of the hole area, a running back comes driving out of the backfield to fire block the defender. This is a tactic intended to confuse the defense.

SLAM BLOCK

There are times when delayed action in the backfield makes it wise to have an offensive lineman delay throwing his block. This kind of block is called a slam block and simply calls for a short jab step with the far foot and a turn toward the direction of the block. Then, count "one thousand one" and go into the block you feel is best suited for the play and the defender.

PULL BLOCK

This block is very similar to the trap block in all but two aspects. The initial movements are the same, but the angle coming away from the pivot is parallel to the line of scrimmage instead of the 45-degree angle of the trap block. The reason is that, on the pull the blocker is heading around the end to lead the interference for the running back. By the time the corner is reached, the blocker usually is able to turn and head downfield. The flat pull down the line of scrimmage is intended to get the blocker to the corner for his turn as fast as possible. The other difference from the trap is that the block on the pull is almost always a downfield cross body block, a review of which follows.

DOWNFIELD CROSS BODY BLOCK

This is one of the most frequently used blocks because there are many players releasing downfield on every running play. The typical situation exists when the ball is going to one side of the field, so the blockers on the other side go downfield to block people in the secondary. Every offensive player must learn to throw this block because they will all have an opportunity, at one time or another, to use it. The best technique requires the blocker to get as close to the defender as possible, two to three feet away, before the block is begun. The blocker should strive to throw his butt into the opponent's chest as his arms swing across the defender's body to make the blocker's body horizontal as it makes contact. His legs end up on one side of the opponent and his arms on the other. Do not be too cautious when going downfield. Just look for a different-colored jersey, get close to it, avoid leaving your feet too soon, and thrust your body into it as hard as you can.

CRACK BACK BLOCK

This block is often referred to as an illegal block by TV commentators when it is thrown by a flanker on a defensive end. In that situation the flanker must get around to the front side of the defensive end and can then throw a variety of shoulder blocks on him above the waist that are legal. The most common one being used now is a shoulder block to avoid having an official call a clip on a questionable cross body block. But there is an important crack back block that is used within the so-called legal clipping area, five yards toward the sideline on either side of where the ball is spotted and three yards toward each goal line. In this area a block front or aft on any defender is considered legal and no penalty will be called. The crack back block is a down block, usually thrown on a linebacker by an on-side lineman who releases on a flat straight line toward the linebacker. The head should be driven in front as the outside shoulder is slammed into the linebacker's hip. The on-side lineman is one who is on the side of the center toward which the ball is being run. Linemen on the other side of the center are referred to as off-side or back-side linemen. The value of this block is that the on-side lineman is sealing off the linebacker by not allowing him to pursue the ball, which is going to his side of the field. This is important because linebackers make most of the tackles, particularly those on their side of the field.

PASS BLOCKING TECHNIQUES

If your coach believes in throwing the ball, you will have to learn how to pass block. This is not a complicated job and can be improved on through constant practice. The air-minded coach will have you work long and hard on your ability because, even if he has a great passer and excellent receivers, they will do him little good if they don't have the time to do their thing.

Most coaches believe that pass blocking is done best from a posture that resembles that of an ape. When an offensive guard and an offensive tackle come out of their three-point stance, they should assume a semicrouch with their knees flexed, their arms hanging loosely at their sides, and their bodies ready to spring forth into

DROP-BACK PASS BLOCKING

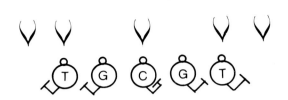

PASS BLOCKING—FIRST STEP

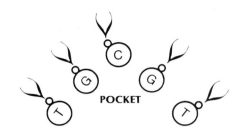

PASS BLOCKING AROUND POCKET

their opponents. If you can visualize an ape walking across his cage, hunched over with a low center of gravity, you will recognize what the pass blocking posture should be.

The first step out of the three-point stance is a backward step with the outside leg opening up (turning) toward the sideline. The outside leg step is used when the coach wants a pocket formed for the quarterback to throw from in the common drop-back type of passing that many teams use. Pass blockers want to encourage defenders to rush toward the outside so the outside step becomes an invitation to the pass rusher to go outside. This maneuver helps create the pocket (see diagram above).

After taking the first step, the pass blocker brings his hands up to his chest with his fists clenched tightly to be ready to deliver his first blow to the defender with his forearms and/or shoulder. As soon as he gets close enough to hit, the blocker must thrust himself out of his crouch and fire up into the rusher's chest to stop his forward momentum and break his stride. The primary goal is to cause him to lose his balance, even hit him hard enough to push him back onto his heels.

As this first blow is completed, the blocker must regain his own balance, drop into his crouch again, shuffle back farther away from the line of scrimmage, and prepare for the next attack. This time the rusher may try to vary his charge. He may try to "swim," with his arms flailing at you, to push your head off to one side and try to destroy your balance. To avoid this approach, you must keep your feet a little farther apart than your shoulders to improve your ability to keep your balance. Another tech-

nique to counter his move is to pop him again, up and through his chest. Do not let him stay close to you. When you thrust at him and make contact, immediately retreat to recover for another thrust. Usually three blows are sufficient for the quarterback to throw the ball, but you should keep blocking until the whistle blows.

Another approach to good pass blocking is to think of your back as a camera and try to keep it focused on the quarterback at all times. Even though you won't always be able to see him, you

With knees flexed, the offensive linemen throw their pass blocks and recover to block again to protect the quarterback.

SPRINT-OUT PASS BLOCKING

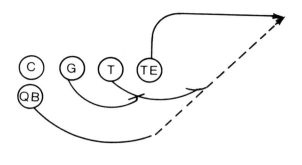

DRAW PLAY PASS BLOCKING

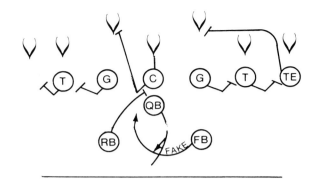

can visualize where he is and you should always try to keep the defender from getting into the picture.

Pass blocking for sprint-out or roll-out passes will require some of the offensive guards and offensive tackles to block as above, but others may have to pull out and back to assume a pass blocking role similar to that of a running back. Getting to the proper area is similar to a trap block release in which you have to take the first step on a 45-degree angle away from the line of scrimmage. When you get to a depth of five yards at a point behind the starting point of the tight end's three-point stance, you will have to turn your shoulders square to the line of scrimmage and then deliver the same blocking technique covered in the drop-back (see diagram above left). A number of drills (covered later) will allow you to improve pass blocking skills.

BLOCKING TECHNIQUES FOR THE DRAW PLAY

A pass-oriented offense will have to use the draw play in order to counter the pass rush that is certain to come from the defense. There are many such plays, but they all have the same theme: to let the defense think that a pass is going to be thrown. Offensive linemen have special blocking tasks to perform if their roles in the draw plays are to be executed properly. Without a good performance by the offensive five, most of the draw plays will be ineffective and the pass offense will suffer as well.

Remember that the draw is supposed to look like a pass play. Therefore, the center, the offensive guards, and the offensive tackles must take the first step exactly as they would on a pass

play. In fact, if they can pass block their men to the outside and ride them out of the play, their execution couldn't be any better (see diagram above right). The key to a successful draw is to encourage the defenders to rush wildly and be ridden out of the way of the running back. However, each blocker must ensure that his opponent doesn't get into the running back's running lane. To do this, they may have to use what is known as a *chop block*. This block simply calls for the blocker, once he no longer can pass block his man out of the way, to throw a cross body block on him and roll through him to take him down. This chopping action is often used on pass plays as well. It is the last resort for a blocker when he is losing his man.

There is also a matter of timing for blocking on draw plays. If the running back is going to run to daylight somewhere in the middle of the line, an offensive tackle, after riding his man to the outside, can release him and head downfield for another block on someone in the secondary. Timing is very important because the offensive guard and offensive tackle cannot release too soon or their opponents may still get to the running back.

BLOCKING FOR PUNTS AND KICKS

In the discussion of line splits, we mentioned that although field goal/extra point teams use no line splits at all, some coaches believe in their use for punts, while others do all their punting from a tight front. The blocking techniques are different to some degree, depending on whether or not line splits are used (see diagram top of page 89).

TWO PUNTING FORMATIONS

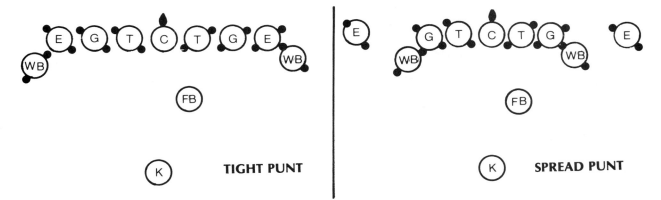

TIGHT PUNT   **SPREAD PUNT**

In the spread punt formation, there is danger of a defender finding a way to get into your backfield to block the punt. This risk is taken because, when you have all your players bunched up in the middle of the field and there is a low punt, with a few blocks on the ends, someone can easily run a punt back for a touchdown against you. By having your people spread out, you have much better coverage across the width of the field and it takes many blocks to spring someone loose against you.

The problem to contend with as a blocker is not allowing anyone free entry to your inside. If an opponent lines up on your head, you can pop him once or twice with a shoulder block and prevent him from blocking the punt. However, if there is also someone in your inside gap, you have to see if your teammate on that side has anyone in his inside gap that he is going to have to block. If so, then you have to ignore the man on you and block the man in the gap. One of the backs will have to pick up your man (see diagram below).

Many coaches are switching to the upright two-point stance for their punting teams. This permits easier delivery of shoulder blocks and

PUNT BLOCKING—INSIDE GAP

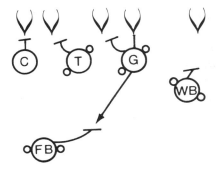

The field goal team's offensive line gives the kicker time to kick a twenty-seven–yard field goal that won the game.

also allows quicker reaction when going down-field to cover the punt. Another technique that is used with the two-point stance is the finger-pointing style. To avoid confusion as to which defender each blocker is going to block, starting at the right end position, each player points at the man he's going to block. This avoids the occasional situation in which two blockers block the same man and another defender gets in with no block put on him at all.

On field goal/extra point blocking, the stand-ard three-point stance is commonly used. The blockers may either be asked to turn their bodies toward the center to form a wall of bodies to prevent penetration or asked to fire out into the crotches of their three-pointed opponents to keep them from getting into the backfield and to keep them low by taking their legs out from under them.

Another blocking style is the two-point stance in which each blocker stands with his hands on his knees with his inside foot six inches farther back from the line of scrimmage than his out-side foot. In this blocking stance, each blocker is

instructed to step up toward the line of scrim-mage with his inside foot when the ball is snapped and to lower his shoulders into the onrushing opponents. As is true in any forma-tion, the inside gap must always be protected first. As long as there is a solid stance to deliver a shoulder block, and as long as the blocker's balance is maintained, there is little difficulty in the blocking performance.

BLOCKING FOR SCREEN PASSES

As was true in the review of blocking for the draw play, the execution of the blocking assign-ments for screen passes includes a number of things that must be done to improve the chances of success. A screen pass usually begins as a pass play and the quarterback tries to eye fake the defense into thinking he's throwing the ball downfield but, at the last second, he dumps the ball off to a running back or other receiver.

In order to get the defensive front out of the way on screen passes, they are encouraged to

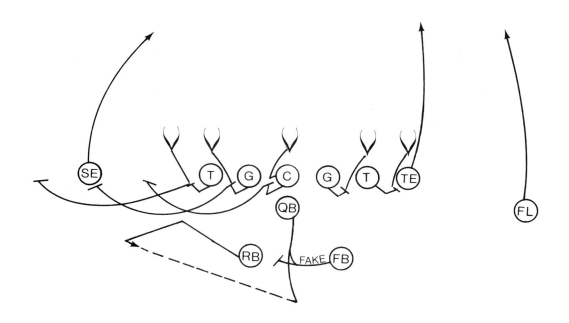

**SCREEN PASS—LINE BLOCKING
BEHIND LOS**

rush in wildly. The best way to do this is to throw very weak blocks at them or no blocks at all. Again, it is a matter of timing because, if they are allowed in too quickly, they may rush the quarterback too much, preventing him from going through his performance, and the play may fail. The best technique, most coaches will agree, is to have the blockers make at least one pop at their men and then release them in a direction that will not interfere with the screen pass. Most screen passes require only one side of the field to be handled in this fashion, which allows the other blockers to go through their normal blocking techniques to protect the quarterback. In addition, the blockers on the screen pass side of the field have to get in front of the receiver to provide him with some blocking assistance after he catches the ball and tries to run downfield (see diagram on page 90).

This used to be a common problem for offensive linemen because the rule formerly said they were not allowed past the line of scrimmage until the pass was completed. Because of a recent rule change, that is no longer necessary and, as long as a pass is completed behind the line of scrimmage, offensive linemen may go beyond the line of scrimmage to put themselves into key locations to block for the receiver downfield (see diagram below). In either arrangement, whether blockers are on one side or the other, there is a need to block people who will react to the pass and rush to stop it. When three blockers are sent out to block, the closest one to the sideline must block the first man in from the sideline; the second blocker takes the next man in; and the third man blocks back toward the center of the field. This generally gives the receiver an opportunity to gain some yardage. These open field blocks can be either shoulder fire blocks or downfield cross body blocks, depending on the location of the defenders and the quickness of the blockers.

Perhaps the most important thing to remember about blocking for screen passes is not to be too anxious to move out to the blocking assignment for the pass receiver. The defense is always alert to easy access into the offensive backfield. Defensive coaches will advise their

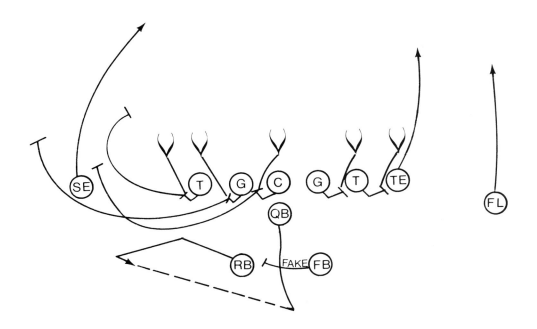

**SCREEN PASS—DOWNFIELD BLOCKING
PAST LOS**

linemen to stop and look for a screen pass if they meet with no resistance from the pass blockers. Therefore, you have to make some contact on your initial blocking thrust and try to let your opponent think that he has gotten around you to rush the quarterback.

Similarly, if the defense sees you quickly re-leasing out toward the flat to block, they will pursue you and knock the pass down, intercept it, or tackle the receiver in your backfield. Be patient and follow your coach's direction well because he has to assure that all the timing requirements for the success of the play are met by every member of the team.

11 | Putting the Passing Game Together

The pro-set formation spreads the receivers toward both sidelines to allow the passing game to attack the entire field or wherever the defense fails to protect.

MULTIPLE FORMATIONS FOR PASSING

Multiple offenses and the passing game go together. There are many different formations that may be used to give the passing offense an advantage in coping with the defenses now being used at all levels of football. They are designed to attack different areas of the defense and to exploit any underprotected part of the field (see diagram on page 94).

The arrangement of receivers and backs has two definite objectives. First, we want to be able to put more than one receiver in any area of the defense; second, we want to force the defense constantly to rearrange their personnel in the hope that they will make a mistake and become confused in their coverage of our personnel. There are many other arrangements that your coach may want to use, but these will give you some of the concepts that are involved.

PASSING FORMATIONS

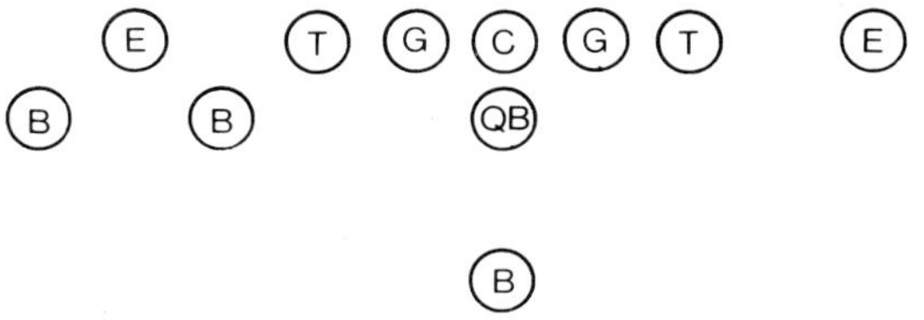

SPREAD—TRIPS LEFT

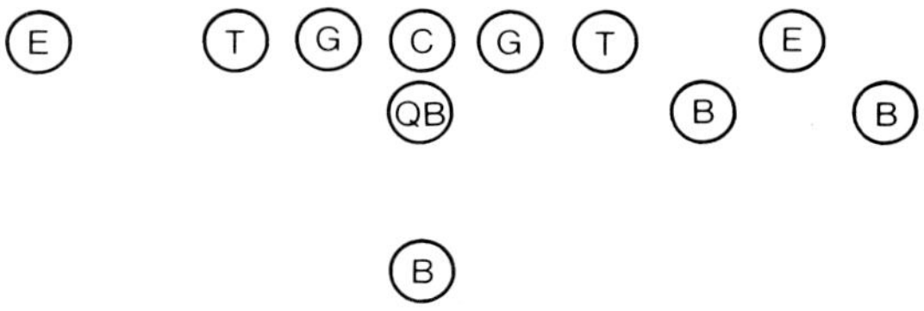

SPREAD—TRIPS RIGHT

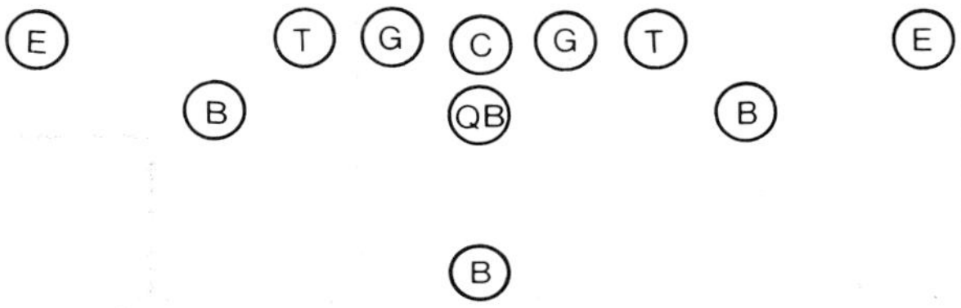

DOUBLE SLOT

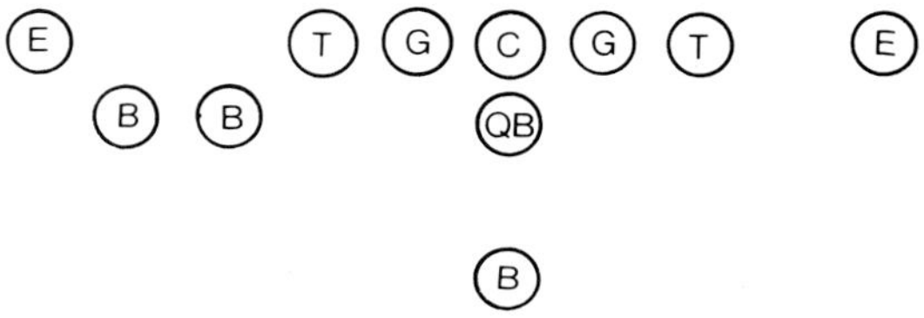

TWINS—SLOT LEFT

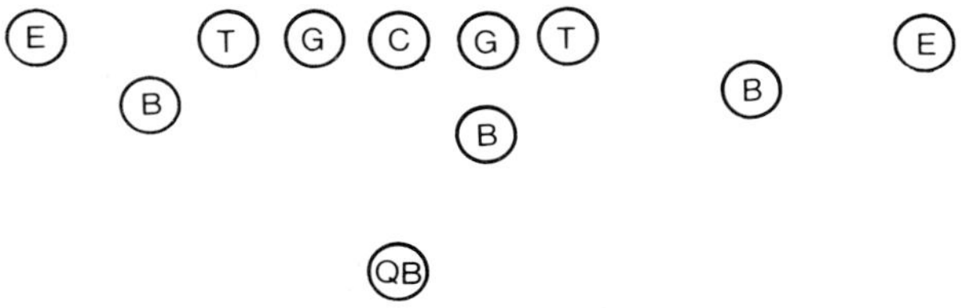

SHOTGUN

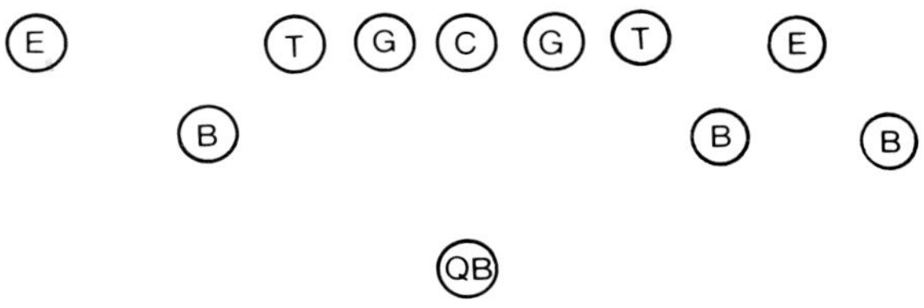

SHOTGUN–TRIPS RIGHT

PASS PATTERNS

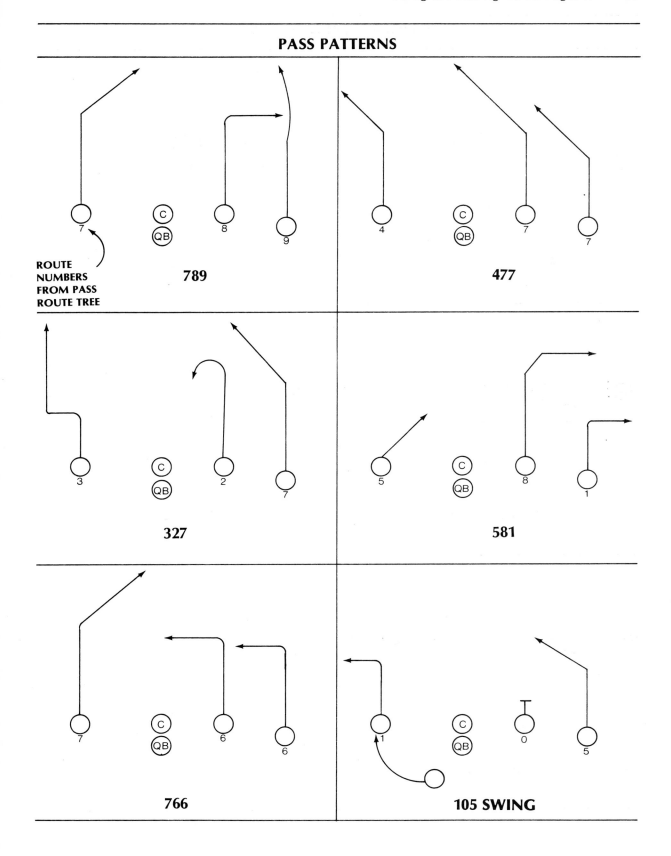

ROUTE
NUMBERS
FROM PASS
ROUTE TREE

789

477

327

581

766

105 SWING

PASS PATTERNS AND ROUTES

Although these terms are used interchangeably, a pass route is the specific way and place that a receiver runs in order to attack an area (or zone) to receive a pass (see diagram on page 95), and a pass pattern is the combination of the routes run by all receivers on a given play. Many different patterns can be arranged into a pass play. Some of them are shown in the diagram.

The purpose of the pass patterns varies somewhat. The coach's game plan has determined that there are places that he wants to be able to attack, so he designs a play that will meet that objective—short or long, left or right, to any receiver.

Some pass plays are designed specifically for one game, and others are used regularly for all games because the coach believes in them and because they have produced good results during his years of experience. A good example of a standard pass that most teams use is the tight end drag pass, which can be run many different ways (see diagram below).

The shotgun allows the offense to put two receivers to each side and can also release a running back on every pass play.

TIGHT END DRAG PASS

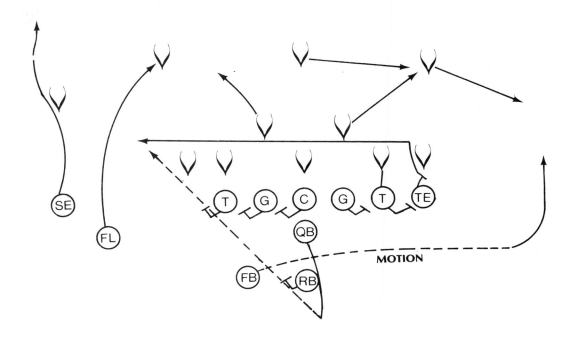

COMBINATION PASS PATTERNS

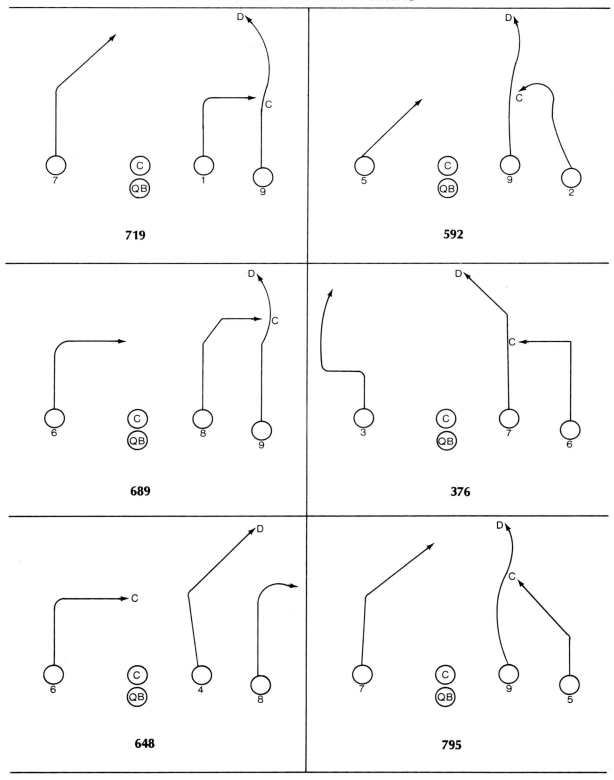

719

592

689

376

648

795

D = DECOY   C = COMBP MAN

By having the twin wide receivers run through the left zone areas, the defenders in that area become occupied with their coverage, linebackers have dropped deep into their hook zones, and the tight end becomes wide open for the reception. This concept of pass patterns is called *combination passes.*

THE USE OF COMBINATION PASSES

When you use one receiver to clear a zone, and you send another receiver into that emptied zone, you have designed a combination pass because you have put two pass routes together for the benefit of one of them. With the wide variety of pass routes available (see diagram on page 95) it is possible to set up an unlimited number of combination pass patterns (see diagram on page 97). Each of these patterns is intended to allow the second man into the zone to be open. It requires two things to happen. The first is that the decoy man must be certain that the defender in the zone covers him. This may be done by running his pass route right through the man, almost running into him if necessary to make sure that he sees and follows him. The decoy must also be careful not to run into someone else's zone, which would permit the defender to let him go and remain in his own zone, thereby fouling up the play.

If the combo man finds that he is being covered man to man, he must use his best moves on his defender to give the quarterback someone to throw to in the emptied zone. It is understandable, then, even if both receivers are covered man to man, that a combination pass can still work; but it is much more effective against zone coverage.

GETTING THE BACKS INTO THE PASS OFFENSE

With the popularity of the multiple offense has come an increase in the use of running backs in the team's pass offense. Many of the formations have moved running backs up closer to the line of scrimmage in a slot or flanker alignment from which they have easy access into the secondary. On most occasions, their pass routes take them into the flat areas because they can get to them quickly and because the other receivers are usually somewhere downfield (see diagram below). A number of things have to be worked out in order to make your passing game to your backs effective. First, pass blocking by the front five has to be good because, when a running back goes out for a pass, there is one less blocker for the quarterback. Second, you have to try to ensure that the back is able to get out of the backfield to run his route. This is not always easy to do when the release is through the crowd doing the pass blocking. Therefore, running backs must look for openings to run through when they run forward, and the quarterback may have to be patient until the back gets open. A typical pass to illustrate this is shown in the diagram at top of page 99. This kind of pass is effective because the linebackers, who cover the running backs on pass plays,

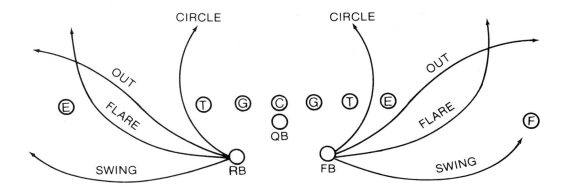

BACK PASS PATTERNS

PRO-RIGHT–FULLBACK CIRCLE

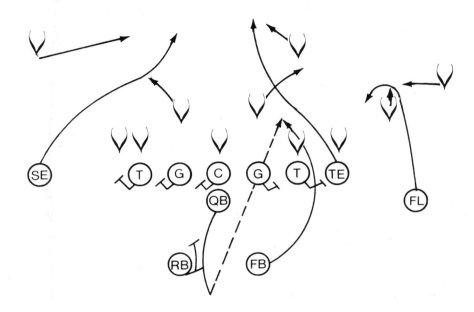

SLOT LEFT—SCREEN LEFT

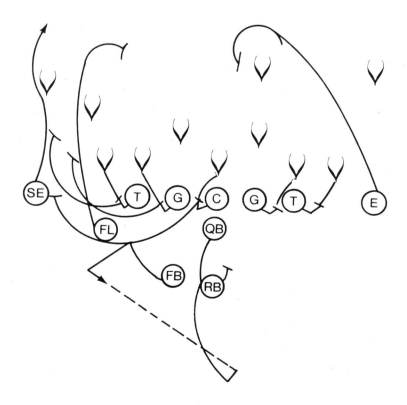

don't find it too easy to see the running back when he is in the crowd in front of the pocket. When the running back gets through, he must look for daylight in the zone to provide a good target for the quarterback.

USE OF SCREEN PASSES

The most frequently heard reason for using screen passes is that they tend to counteract a strong pass rush and can burn the defense when they stunt their linebackers too often. These observations are true, but screen passes also attack the weak flat zone and, if executed well with an elusive running back, can pick up some big chunks of yardage. One commonly used screen pass is shown in the diagram (see bottom of page 99). After the quarterback fakes a draw to the running back, the running back blocks. The front right offensive linemen do their normal pass blocking and the quarterback eye fakes to the wide receiver out in the right flat. All of this is done to draw the defense's attention away from the left flat. The wide receiver on the left must take his man deep to get him away from the pass area; the left side offensive tackle, offensive guard, and center make their quick pop pass blocks and release out for their second blocking assignments on the play.

While all of these things are happening, the running back who will receive the pass must step up as though he were setting up to pass block. As he crouches down and and raises his arms to his chest in typical pass blocking form, he must take short steps through the onrushing

The quarterback completes the screen pass left as the offensive linemen rush out to help the running back get downfield.

defenders and sneak out into the flat. Then he should turn around partially to face the quarterback and raise his arms to show the quarterback where he is. As soon as he catches the ball, he must shout "Go" to let his blockers know that they can begin to throw the blocks that will allow him to move downfield. The entire play requires many people to do many things well, but the extra weapon that screen passes give an offense are certainly worth it.

WHEN TO USE DROP-BACK AND SPRINT-OUT PASSES

There are, a few general views that apply to the use of drop-back versus sprint-out passes. The ability of the quarterback is one of the decision makers because, if he fits into the coach's running plans, the sprint-out pass enables him to add another dimension to the team's offense. When he comes rushing out around end, if the defenders don't know whether he's going to pass or run, they are forced to try to cover both, usually giving an advantage to the

offense (see diagram below). The defense's left cornerback and left safety must make a decision as to whether to come up and play the run or stay back and cover against the pass.

If the quarterback is not a runner, or if the team is blessed with a very good throwing quarterback and some good receivers, the drop-back pass approach has many benefits to support its use. This system can attack the entire field, not just half of the field as is true of the sprint-out approach. This forces the defense to protect the entire field and makes the multiple offense more effective because its strength is to attack anywhere on the field.

Drop-back also gives you many more draw play and screen pass possibilities because on any given play they may be used to the left, to the right, and also in the middle of the field. Throwing to the backs is also possible anywhere on the field.

HIGH PERCENTAGE PASS PLAYS—PLAY ACTION

When long yardage is required to make a first down, you should have some plays available

SPRINT-OUT PASS-RUN OPTION

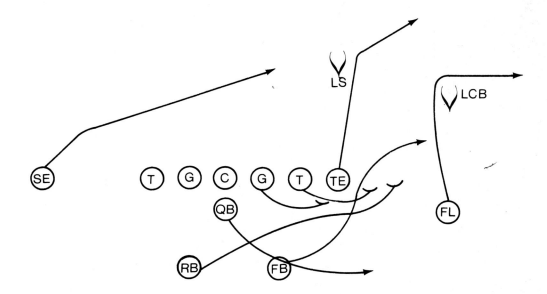

that are almost sure to be successful. High-percentage pass plays, coming with play action fakes, usually provide this kind of weapon. If a given play brings success time after time, it deserves to be called a high-percentage play.

Play action is a term that means that before the quarterback throws the ball he must fake to a running back to make the defense think it is a running play. If the fake is done well, the defense will freeze and the pass receiver will have an advantage as he discreetly runs his pass route. A favorite play action pass is shown in the diagram below. All the fakes must be prolonged, exaggerated fakes to really mislead the defense. Only one receiver is sent out because, if more were to release, the secondary would become wary and then look for a pass. The receiver must run to daylight quickly but not after he has thrown a quick, fake block to hide the pass. The quarterback has the key faking role to play. First, he must really put the ball into the running back's midsection to make the fake more realistic; second, he must hide the ball as he turns and "looks off" the defense before he delivers the ball.

The quarterback fakes to the running back as the offensive linemen take their pass-blocking positions on a play action pass.

I-SLOT LEFT—FLAT PASS

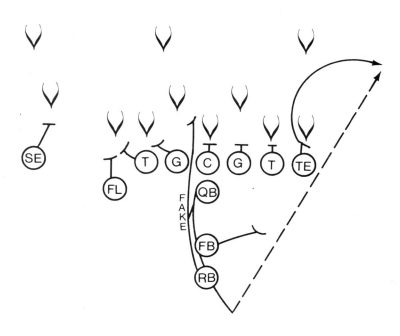

The team listens to the quarterback call the play in their pass-oriented huddle that allows receivers to go to their set positions on either side of the field.

Use of the Huddle in the Pass Offense

The huddle is a vital part of any offensive scheme, but its arrangement for the passing offense can help achieve the success a team always seeks. Because of the multiple sets that a pass offense uses, the receivers and the running backs go to many different locations on the field in order to take their set positions. To make their exit from the huddle as simple as possible, and at the same time to avoid giving the defense any more information than is absolutely necessary, a good huddle arrangement is essential (see diagram at right).

The first requirement of a huddle is that everyone hear the play and the snap sound. The next is that everyone get in and out of the huddle with little confusion and effort. In this arrangement, the center and both ends are closest to the line of scrimmage. The center can get to the ball quickly to get his hands set on it, and the ends can release to either side of the ball

HUDDLE ARRANGEMENT

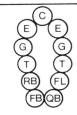

BALL   **LOS**

5 YARDS

without bumping into any of their teammates. This allows them to run quickly to their set positions and forces the defense to rush their alignment as well. The guards and tackles are next, and they can crisscross to the left or right of the center if the multiple formations require them to be strong-side or weak-side players. The strong side is always the one on which the tight end is lined up.

The next pair are the flanker and the running back because they also line up on either side of the field and can move out of the huddle as quickly. Their location on the field also has a bearing on how the defense lines up. Finally, the quarterback and the fullback are at the back of the huddle because the quarterback is always in the middle of the field and the fullback is there more often than any other back. The emphasis on the entire huddle has to be to do things quickly and efficiently and to hustle out to get the play off to a good start, without giving the defense any advantages.

12 | Defensive Philosophy and Strategy

THE MULTIPLE DEFENSE PHILOSOPHY

Many people believe that defense follows offense and that after coaches find new ways to score, defenses are created to stop them. There is no doubt that many new offensive schemes have been put together over the last thirty or so years. And, one by one, the imaginative and smart coaches who run their team's defenses have found a variety of ways to stop them.

The process is still going on and every year a new struggle is seen at either the higher levels of college ball or in the NFL. At this writing, the Dallas Cowboys of the NFL have been the most innovative offensive football team in the country. Therefore it is hardly a surprise that they are up with the leaders of new ideas on defense as well. Understandably, then, they have been at the top or near the top of the NFL for many years. They are always looking for new ways to improve.

An NFL defense geared to stop the offense's running attack, usually used on first down.

105

An NFL defense geared to stop the offense's passing attack, usually used on third or certain pass downs.

More than thirty years ago, most teams had only one offensive formation from which they both ran and passed out of. Any team defending them only needed one defense to handle them and both phases of the game were simple and uncomplicated. Now, with many teams having so many different offensive sets, it is very difficult, almost impossible, to defend against them all with only one defensive alignment.

Therefore, the multiple defense approach to the game was born out of necessity, to give a team an opportunity to meet and cope with the new thrusts coming at them. But the defensive coaches did not want to overcomplicate their situation by using too many different defenses, so they generally have tried to use a few basic defenses with a variety of alternatives. At the same time they were prepared to make special adjustments specifically for the game coming at them each week, based on the scouting reports. To the offenses it meant that you could count on some special things that you may not have seen your opponent do in your scouting of them. It has all become a matter of philosophy (or what you believe in) and strategy (or what you are going to do about it).

A VARIETY OF FORMATIONS

There are some well-known basic defenses that many teams use, whether it be at the youth, high school, or college level. They are commonly used in much the same manner (see diagram on page 107). They break down into what are called odd and even formations. Odd are those defenses in which a man is playing on the

An odd 5-2-4 defense that is one of the most popular all-purpose defenses used in high school and college.

DEFENSIVE FORMATIONS
VS
PRO RIGHT

| ODD | EVEN |

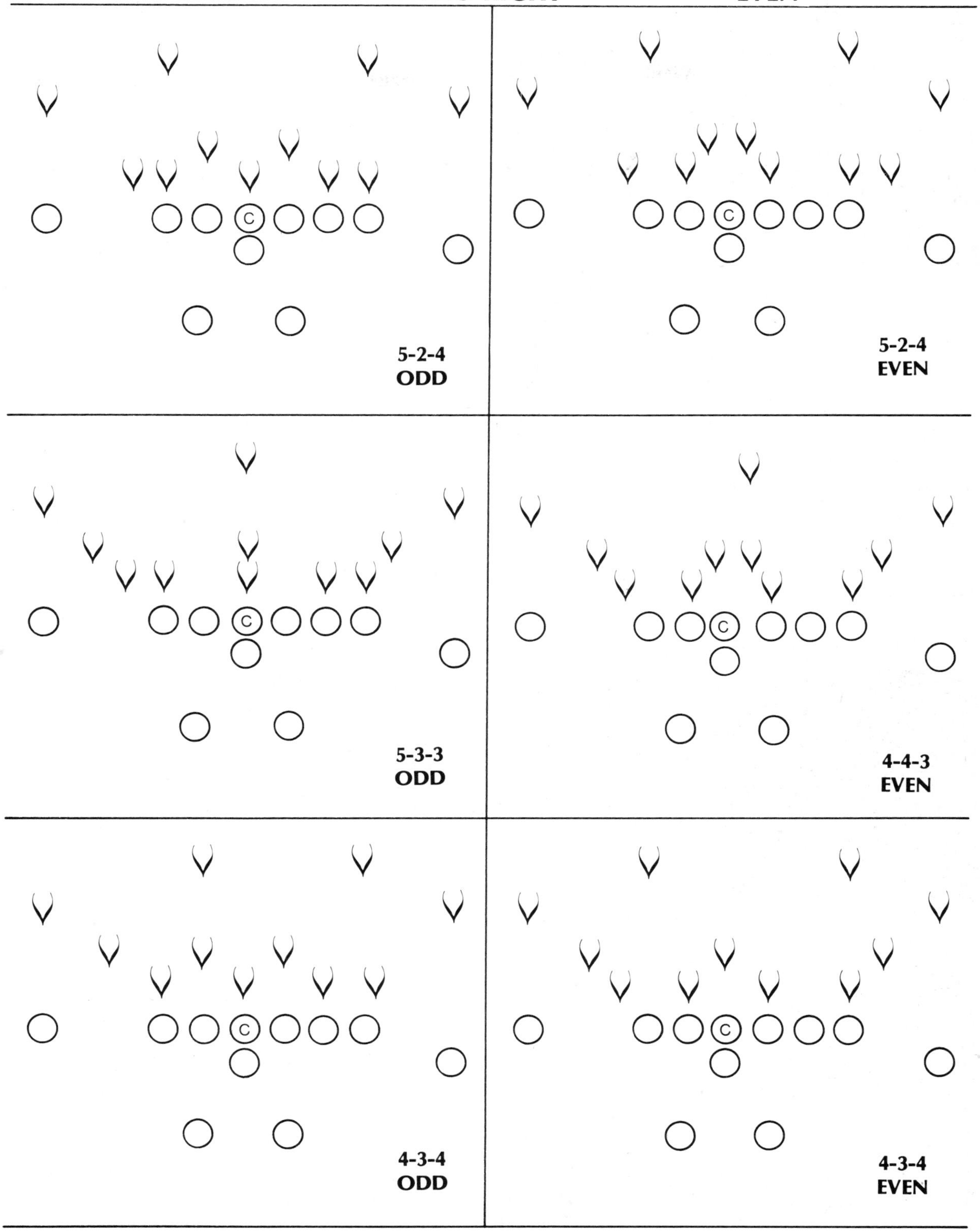

5-2-4
ODD

5-2-4
EVEN

5-3-3
ODD

4-4-3
EVEN

4-3-4
ODD

4-3-4
EVEN

DEFENSIVE FORMATIONS
VS
ODD   OTHER OFFENSES   EVEN

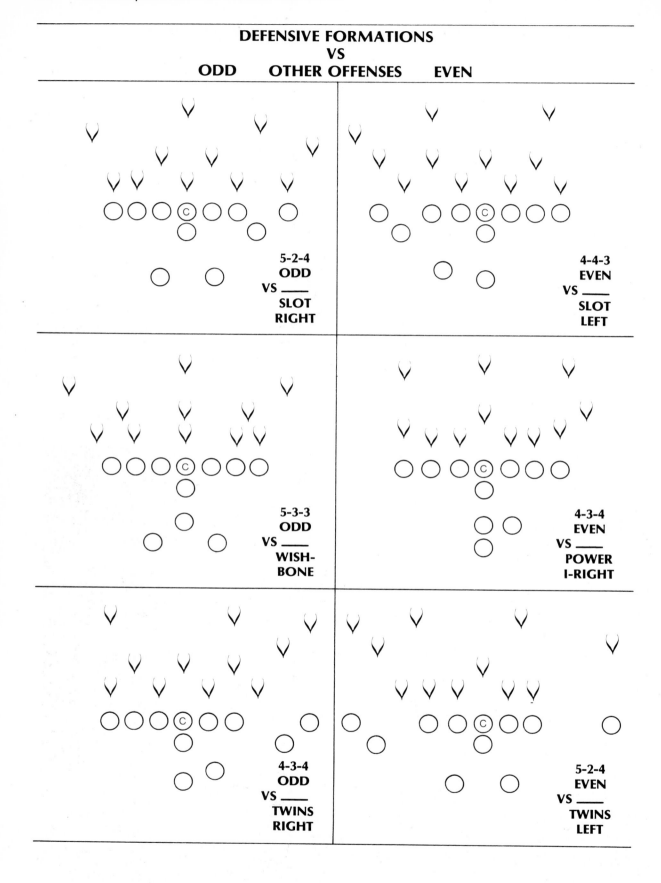

5-2-4 ODD VS ___ SLOT RIGHT

4-4-3 EVEN VS ___ SLOT LEFT

5-3-3 ODD VS ___ WISHBONE

4-3-4 EVEN VS ___ POWER I-RIGHT

4-3-4 ODD VS ___ TWINS RIGHT

5-2-4 EVEN VS ___ TWINS LEFT

center on the line of scrimmage because they are most often aligned that way in the five-man front. If the center is uncovered, the defense is referred to as an even defense because it is most often used in a four- or six-man arrangement on the line of scrimmage. These basic odd and even number sets have been modified and adjusted in countless ways, usually by merely changing the places where certain players line up. And, as mentioned above, they are changed because a change may make the basic defense more suitable for a particular opponent. Let's look at some of these versus some slightly different offensive formations (see diagram on page 108).

If you look closely, you'll see that some movement has occurred both on the line of scrimmage and in the secondary because the strength of the offensive formation was shifted from right to left. Without the adjustments, the offense would have more horsepower in one area or another, thus gaining an advantage over the defense.

HOW TO CONFUSE THE OFFENSE

Some defensive coaches are content to sit back and counter what the offense does. Their attitude is that whatever the offense does to them, they will find a way to handle it and avoid embarrassment. This concept leaves it up to the offense to try to fool or confuse the defense, and when it does, some points may be put on the scoreboard.

In another school, the coaches do not enjoy waiting to see something new, but prefer to take matters into their own hands by changing things around to confuse the offense. That is, they take the offense, so to speak, and launch their strategy to stop the offense.

The most common way this is done is to change their alignment to a new formation that the offense may not be prepared to block; or they may add a number of stunts to their basic defenses. Of the two, the stunts are more popular because they don't require as much reeducation

An adjustment of the five-man defense is to have the weak side tackle (left) move over and "eagle" toward the strong side of the offense, or the wide side of the field.

5-2 DEFENSIVE FORMATIONS

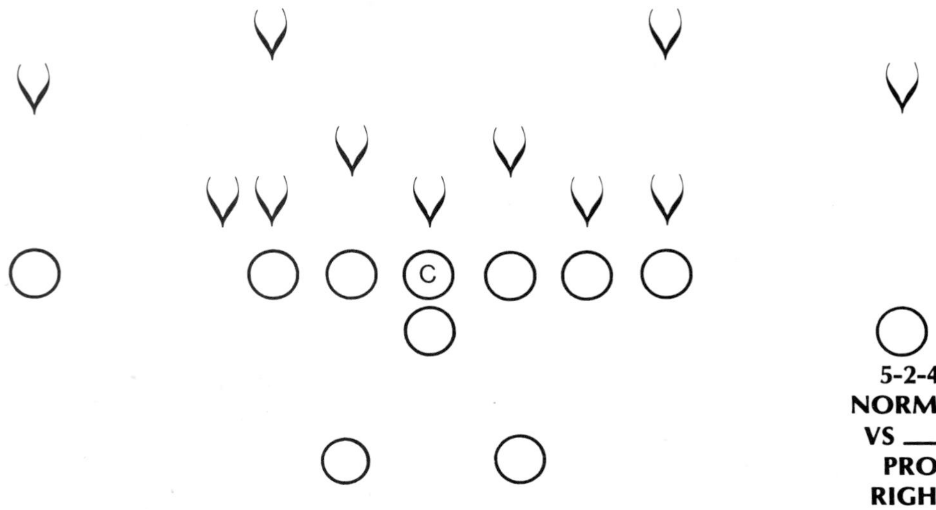

5-2-4
NORMAL
VS ____
PRO
RIGHT

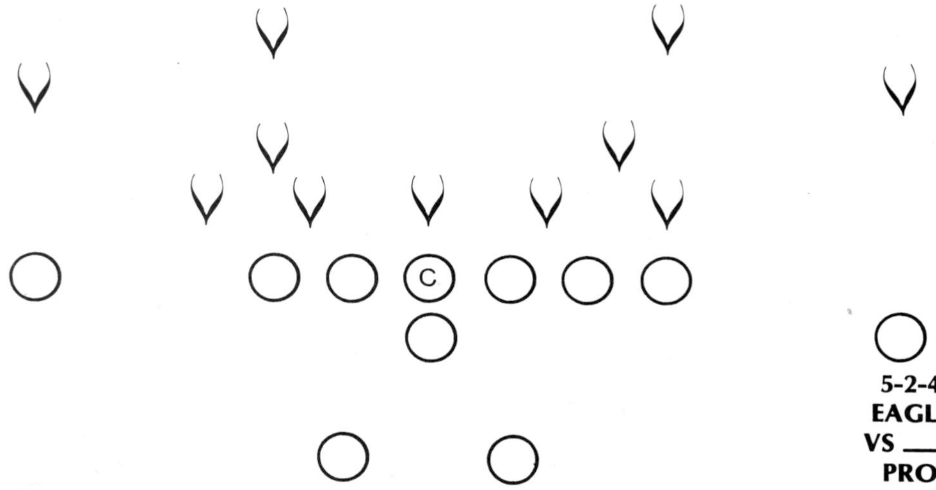

5-2-4
EAGLE
VS ____
PRO
RIGHT

of the players. However, good offensive teams have been trained to cope with stunts and they alone may not be enough to do the trick for you. Therefore, many coaches are going to a variety of formations right from the beginning of the season to give their players more time to learn all the differences between one formation and the other (see diagram above). Many different adjustments can be made through the use of stunts. They will be covered in detail in the sections on defensive linemen and linebackers (see chapters 13 and 14), but we would like to review how and why they are done to confuse the offense.

THE USE OF STUNTS AND GAMES

Some people have a misconception that stunts, games, and blitzes are only done by linebackers. On the contrary, any member of the defense can and often is involved in one or many ways. The purpose of these special actions is to give the offense a condition that they are not prepared for or that fouls up the area of the field that the offense may be attacking. Done well, it can throw an offense off balance; in the right situation, it can also stop a long drive down the field.

LINEBACKER STUNTS

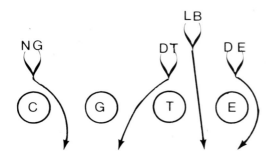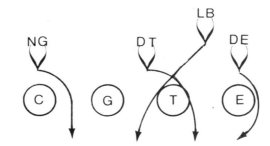

To review a few tactics that are often used, look at the diagram above. Timing is a very important part of stunting well. In the first example, the linebackers must get across the line of scrimmage at the snap of the ball so that they and the defensive tackles are attacking at the same time. If there is a delay and they start too late, the offensive guards and offensive tackles may be able to slip off their men and get the linebackers.

In the second example, the down linemen must make their move across the heads of their opponents in order to occupy them so they cannot react quickly to pick up the linebackers going in on the other side.

Imagine what confusion would result if the play were heading for the heart of a defensive attack area. There would be a pile of bodies and no daylight. Also imagine that it is third down and short yardage for a key first down. The play would probably fail, the first down would be missed, and the ball would have to be given up. This is a situation that repeats itself hundreds of times every week across the nation.

BASIC CONCEPTS OF DEFENSE

One of the most frequently heard concepts of defense is to try to take away from the offense the things they do best. If their strength is the passing game, their ability must be curtailed, either through stunts or good coverage. If they run the ball better, then perhaps the line of scrimmage must be overloaded to meet power with power. It may be necessary to take chances to do this, but it may be the only way you can be successful. Start with your normal strategy, but be prepared to open up and change if need be.

Another vital concept of defense is to develop pride in your defensive unit. It is a great morale builder to see the unit in their huddle before the start of each play, calling the defensive formation, holding hands as a sign of unity, and encouraging each other to meet their responsibilities to each other and to the team. Defensive statistics have been kept by more teams than ever before to give their players the recognition they so richly deserve.

Communications for offensive activity started a long time before this technique was used for defensive adjustments. In the past, only offensive spotters were in the press box, but now

The defense adjusts to overload the side of the field that has the twin receivers to counter the offensive team's strength with theirs.

there are defensive spotters as well to pass on vital information about what the offense may be doing successfully against your defense and how they are doing it.

Defenses are now ready to do it all to cope with and keep up with any offense they face. But they must be alert to the dangers of taking some ill-advised chances at the wrong time in the wrong part of the field. There are some basic dos and don'ts that should be discussed.

For example, don't stay with a defensive formation that is not holding its own with your opponent's offense. Do something different to throw them off balance, but change something. Respect the other team's strength. If they have an exceptionally fast wide receiver, instruct your cornerback to play off the line of scrimmage and be willing to give him the short pass, but don't let them hit him with a long bomb. Mistakes that can be chalked up to poor strategy can bring a team's morale down and things may go from bad to worse. Depressed players play poorly.

Don't allow your team to be surprised. If you are a defensive end, don't overpursue a play going around the other end, only to be taken by a reverse that comes back around your end for a big gain. If you are a down lineman and you see

a draw play starting, call out, "Draw" so your teammates are also warned about it. A good defense helps itself out by talking to each other about what is happening or what could be happening on a given play in a certain part of the field. Communicate, encourage, and pat your teammate on the back—and do your part to win. Remember that many games are won by outstanding defensive play. "If they don't score, they can't win" is the defense's slogan.

SELECTING DEFENSIVE PERSONNEL

The quality of players on defense must be at least as good if not better than those on offense. You hear more and more about coaches who pick their defensive players before they choose offensive players. They are realizing that many special skills are necessary for a good defense. There may be many players who can run with the ball with little to choose from between them; but there may not be many who can bring an opponent down in an open field to prevent a touchdown.

If there are at least two special qualities that a defense needs, they have to be speed and toughness. Without really fast players in the sec-

The defensive line charges forward to meet fire power with fire power to stop the offense's strength.

ondary, the entire pass defense will be at a disadvantage when some fleet wide receivers come flying downfield for a pass. It is not surprising to see a coach put his fastest players on the defensive unit.

It goes without saying that the size requirements of both offense and defense are about equal. If you don't meet fire power with fire power, you will get blown out. But not all big players are as tough as others and, if you're not tough, the offense will run over you. A down lineman can't take a backward step because he may end up on his back. There is no greater thrill than to see a tough defensive tackle fight off a double team block and make the big tackle. It can't be done without toughness.

There is also a need for smart players on defense. They must be able to size up what's happening and be smart enough to react quickly to make the stop. And it is not just the linebackers who have to think because every member of the defense is engaging in his own private war. If you can't outmuscle your man, you may be able to outsmart him and gain your advantage that way. Defensive coaches will do everything they can to point out every possible technique for using your head to beat your opponent.

DEFENSIVE SKILLS TRAINING

Each position on a team requires maximum speed from each of its players. Therefore, running has to be a vital part of your defensive training program. As is true of offensive training, the players who play in the secondary have to build up their sprint capability if they are going to cover the fast offensive receivers. A regular diet of sprints every day during preseason will help the cornerbacks and safeties increase their speed.

Most players now use a scheme in which they sprint forty yards and jog forty yards. At first, two of each should be run with a rest in between; then three of each and four of each are run in successive weeks. This will not only build speed; it will also build the endurance that is so necessary in the last quarter of a game.

The big defensive people should follow the same routine that offensive interior linemen use, as reviewed earlier. This stresses endurance ahead of sprinting speed but includes some sprinting, too. Of course, strength training is very important to the big players, and weights and other universal gym techniques should be used. Upper body strength is particularly important to defensive tackles and defensive ends because it helps with their pass rushing ability.

Three defenders use their speed to pursue the running back and get in on the tackle.

The linebacker makes a bear hug tackle as he and the defensive back sack the quarterback at the end of a stunt.

But leg strength is also important to provide the drive to complement the upper body actions.

There must, of course, be constant tackling practice in order to make good tacklers out of everyone on defense. Once you are shown how to tackle—come in low, with your head up, eyes open, knees flexed, and arms hanging ready to clasp the running back—your coach can evaluate your skill and give you good advice on how to improve. He can also tell if you have some ability to react quickly to the movement of the running back and if you are willing to "stick your head in," an expression that means you have no fear of tackling, which is necessary in order to be a good tackler.

Defensive personnel must learn many special techniques that are unique to their positions; these will be dealt with in later chapters. Take time to learn them well and ask your coach for his direction on how he wants you to perform them.

Defensive players are not second-class citizens and must hold up their end of the team. As is true of offensive linemen, you may not get the public's recognition of your talent, but you will have the satisfaction of knowing that the team can't win without you, and that should be all the incentive you need to be a good performer.

13 | Defensive Linemen—The Up-Front Gang

In our review of offensive linemen, it was pointed out that they are usually unknowns on the field. In the NFL the only time you may learn their names is when they are guilty of some rule infraction and the referee calls out their number on the public address system. However, this is not generally true of defensive linemen because they are getting as much recognition as anyone except perhaps the quarterbacks, running backs, and wide receivers.

With the growing emphasis on defense, they have acquired their own fans, who would rather watch the defense stop the other team than see their own team score. And when a big defensive tackle or defensive end gets in to sack the quarterback, bedlam breaks loose in the stands.

How to Choose Interior Linemen

As stated earlier, defensive linemen have to be the big people on the team. They must have the mental toughness that makes them want to come back, play after play, to take the best the offensive linemen have to offer. They must not be concerned with pain other than to make sure they inflict it rather than take it. When a coach looks over his big players, he should single out those with a strong desire to mix it up physically.

In personality, these players must be leaders, those who want to be out front leading the charge. They must feel proud to stand up under the attacks that come their way, not the type who quits when things get tough. Every team has them because this trait almost always accompanies the desire to play football. A term often used to describe these players is *hardnosed*, meaning that they can stick their heads in and take it. The skill requirements must include the ability to tackle. The coach will usually evaluate his big players based on blocking and tackling, the basic skills of the game.

For most, the ability to block well is rarer because tackling is almost instinctive. It is typical to find more boys who tackle well then block well; but some boys tackle with more vigor and hit harder. They are the ones who will often do the best job.

PHYSICAL REQUIREMENTS

There are just so many ways to say that being big is not all that is necessary to play on either side of the line of scrimmage. When you come right down to it, the players who do the most to build up their strength and speed are the ones who excel. This applies to all age groups, whether you are age twelve in junior high or twenty-two in college or anywhere in between. It must be done to stay ahead of the crowd.

Strength is not something that lasts forever. It must be worked on constantly or it will diminish with time. This is often a surprise to young players who stop their weights program for a number of months only to find that they can't press as much as they could have when they stopped. If you want to be at your best, you have to make a commitment to follow a successful course for the development of your skills.

All big people are better if they are quick and if they can get from one place to another in minimum time. The same requirements that apply to the offense also apply to the defense. Your coach will lean toward the players who can move faster if all other things are equal.

DEVELOPING YOUR STRENGTH NEEDS

There is no limit to how much strength you can use while playing these positions. Regardless of your size and body structure, it can be built up and expanded by surprising amounts. It is not uncommon for a boy weighing 190 pounds on a 6'2" frame in high school to put on 40 to 50 pounds of muscle and girth after a few years of continuous weight training. It follows that if that young man suddenly stops his whole buildup program, he may return to 190 pounds after a few years. The point is simple. You will be pleasantly surprised when you see what your body can become if you stay with it.

Through the use of weights, both bars and universals, every part of your body can be strengthened. Get the guidance of your coach and set goals to strive for, but don't make them too severe to start with. Here again, there is literature available to give you an idea of what you can do over periods of time. It is up to you to follow the program faithfully because no one can make you do it successfully if you don't want it yourself.

AGILITY AND QUICKNESS

Agility has been reviewed in many chapters of this book. To smaller athletes it seems to come more readily because their bodies are not as big and heavy. It is a lot easier to be light on your feet if you are fifty pounds lighter than one of the big interior linemen. But these big linemen can improve their agility and quickness with the same drills that the offensive people use to improve their skills. Running through the tires, ropes, or plastic tubes, as seen in the diagram on page 22, will give the bulky linemen the same kind of practice that the running backs and wide receivers use and will give them the same kind of improvement in proportion to their size.

Another really good device for the improvement of these skills is the jump rope. It is something that can be used the year round when you are all by yourself and it will be as good as anything you can do for yourself.

When the team practices begin, the coach will make the whole team run backward and do other similar body control–type exercises that will give you better coordination. Most of these will be covered in the section on practice (see chapter 17).

STANCE, FOOTWORK, AND TECHNIQUES

The defensive lineman's stance is considerably different from that of the offensive lineman. This is true because on offense the players must be prepared to go forward, sideward, or backward and therefore must have a more balanced stance. This is controlled mainly by the placement of the forward hand. The farther forward it is placed, the more the body is committed to go forward.

The defensive linemen come out of their stances and charge forward as the defensive back reads his key.

On defense, the direction of the charge is always forward, although sometimes on an angle to the left or right in addition to going straight ahead and through the opponent. Therefore, it is not only possible to put the forward hand farther forward; it is also strongly recommended. In fact, to make sure that the

The two defensive linemen stay low and get ready to thrust themselves across the line of scrimmage on the snap of the ball.

defensive linemen stay low and make a strong thrust into the blockers, many coaches direct their down linemen to get into a four-point stance. This calls for the player to put both hands down and to get his feet dug in well behind him to provide a solid base from which to launch.

This technique is most often used in a goal line defense, in which a lineman can't afford to be straightened up or he will be driven out of his area and a touchdown will result. But a four-point stance is also often used by a nose guard from one goal line to another. Some defensive tackles use this same technique because coaches generally agree that they are more difficult to block when they stay low. Their center of gravity is lower and they tend to get under the charge of the offensive lineman. The technique of attack must vary if a defensive tackle or defensive end is going to be successful in his battle with his blocker. In this regard, his entire body comes into play because he must use his hands and arms to ward off the block, his shoulder and upper body to lean into and overcome the blocker's strength, and his legs and feet to drive and guide his body's maneuvers.

The most difficult situation a defensive line-

The defensive end (number 81) chucks his blocker and rushes past him to get into the offensive backfield.

man faces is the double team block of the offensive guard and offensive tackle or offensive tackle and tight end. The blockers will try to combine their shoulders to double their force on the defensive tackle. But, if the defender stays low and tries to split them, he may be able to keep from being driven out of his hole. The double team block may come at him from either side as the offense may try to block him in or out from the center (see diagram below).

Learning how to use your hands and arms is another skill that must be developed. You are not allowed to close your hand to hold your blocker's body or equipment, but you are permitted to push and pull him, forward or backward or from side to side, in order to control him. These tools will help you keep him off your body as he tries to get a shoulder into your chest. As you come up out of your stance, try to straighten up your blocker's body and drive him back to overcome his momentum. This can be done by delivering a forearm shiver, which is an upward stroke of your down arm into the blocker's chest or head and must be quickly followed with your other hand to the shoulder or head. While this is happening, your forward lean and churning legs will continue the thrust into the offensive backfield.

BEATING THE DOUBLE TEAM BLOCK

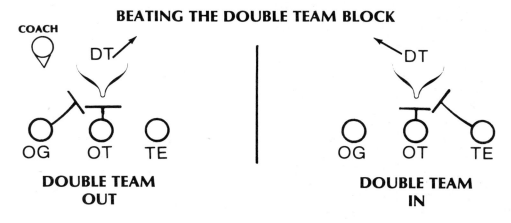

COACH

DT

OG   OT   TE

**DOUBLE TEAM
OUT**

DT

OG   OT   TE

**DOUBLE TEAM
IN**

DEFENSIVE REACTION

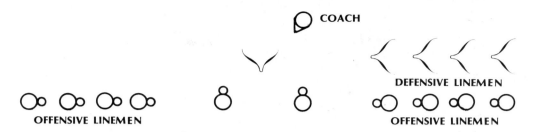

A quick-moving defensive tackle plays off his blocker and prepares to make the tackle on the running back coming at him.

The defensive tackle's drive and churning legs get him into the offensive backfield for a key tackle.

OUTSMARTING YOUR OPPONENT

Techniques like this can be learned best through the use of a variety of drills to simulate game conditions. Because offensive running plays come inside, outside, or through a down lineman, you must be taught to expect an attack from any direction. A good way to prepare for this is to do the drill in the diagram above. By lining up two offensive linemen on either side of the nose guard, defensive tackle, or defensive end, the coach will give them both offensive and defensive practice at the same time. The coach will stand behind the defensive man and will give a hand signal to indicate whether one or the other or both of the offensive players will block the defender. He will also hold up his fingers to indicate the snap sound and then call the sounds as though he were the quarterback to help them go off the mark together. The defender must use a variety of tactics to avoid being blocked.

He may try to dive in between them and come up scrambling to get on his feet and into the backfield. Or he may try to angle his attack into just one opponent to try to beat one man and not two. He may also try a hit-and-spin tactic whereby he drives into the inside shoulder of one man and spins his body in between them as he pushes them apart with his hands.

Another good drill that helps both offensive as well as defensive personnel is the trap drill (see diagram on page 120). By lining up two dummies as though they were the on-side offensive guard and offensive tackle, the off (or other) offensive guard pulls out and comes behind the center and both dummies to meet the defensive tackle as he penetrates the backfield area. The defender must lower his inside shoulder and

Defensive tackle (number 54) takes an angle approach to get through the offensive line, using strength and speed.

turn to meet the attack as he digs in with his outside leg to avoid being driven out of the area. A wise down lineman will drop to a low crouch any time he is being allowed into the backfield because, whenever this is done, he almost always is being set up for a trap from the inside.

Another drill is best suited to the nose guard. When he lines up on the center, he often has uncovered offensive guards on either side of the center, who may also be anxious to block him (see page 121, diagram at left). This drill will help train the offensive guards to do their down blocks on the nose guard. By having the center actually center the ball, the nose guard has an opportunity to move with the ball, a skill that he must develop well in order to play this difficult position. He must try a number of techniques to avoid the blockers. By quickly putting his hands on the center's shoulders, he may go around him into the backfield before either offensive guard can get to him. The hit and spin is another good tactic to use because the center is occupied with centering the ball to the quarterback and may not be quick enough to recover. A common nose guard trick is to pull the center forward as he snaps the ball because, when the ball is raised up and back to the quarterback, his balance is slightly off and he is vulnerable.

FIGHTING THE TRAP BLOCK

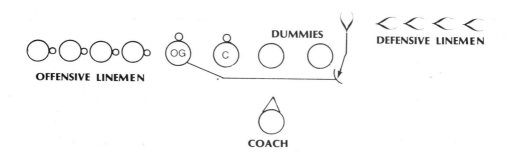

The defensive end (number 87) broke the block with his inside shoulder and rushes at the quarterback to stop the play.

The defensive end must learn to cope with an inside out block from an offensive tackle, a heads-up block by a tight end, or a down block by a tight flanker. To familiarize him with these various problems, a special drill is often used by many teams (see diagram bottom right). Once again, the coach stands behind the defenders and points at the offensive man with whom he wants to block the defensive end. Again, the snap sound is shown with the coach's fingers and the snap sounds are called. All the techniques mentioned earlier should be tried by the defensive end but, because of the flanker being off the line of scrimmage, he may do another thing. Namely, he may make his charge into the flanker and then turn in toward the middle of the field to look for the ball. By staying low with his inside shoulder, he is in position to fight off a block by a running back and jam up the area.

NOSE GUARD REACTION DRILLS

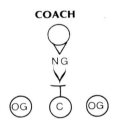

BLOCK STRAIGHT

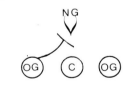

BLOCK RIGHT

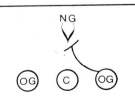

BLOCK LEFT

DEFENSIVE END REACTION DRILLS

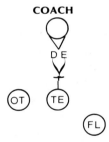

BLOCK STRAIGHT

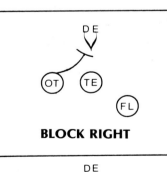

BLOCK RIGHT

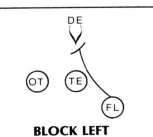

BLOCK LEFT

The nose guard uses his hands and forearm to play off the center and be ready for the ball if it comes at him.

TRAINING TO DEVELOP SKILLS

The skills that must be developed are typical of those covered in the preceding drills and in those in chapter 17. In many of these you can beat on dummies instead of players. The thing to do is to get a few of your teammates in the preseason period and, with the use of some dummies, set up some defensive linemen stance-and-drive drills. One player holds a dummy and the other takes his stance, fires off, and explodes into it.

With merely a helmet and shoulder pads, a pass rushing exercise can be set up with which to practice your pass rush. The swim technique that was mentioned in the section on offensive linemen can be developed in this kind of setup. You can also try the pass rush tactic in which you drive to the inside of the blocker and then spin off to his outside as you push off with your hands and forearms. You can also work on your "up from under" style, which calls for you to shiver with both your hands under the pass blocker's shoulders. Once you have straightened him up, you keep pushing him back on his heels and keep him off balance. Once he is off balance, you own him.

As important as size is, technique is of equal importance. You have to learn many ways of dealing with your blockers. If you come at them with only your strength and desire, you may

Defensive tackle (number 73) pushed his blocker off balance and rushes the passer with his arm up to block the pass.

succeed from time to time but not as often as you will if you develop the skills to go along with your strength. Also remember that you have to use your head, too, because you must determine what is the best technique to use in various situations. By studying your opponent's style, you can determine what he likes to do in certain situations and you have to counteract them.

14 | Linebackers--The Heart of the Defense

Of all the defensive positions, linebackers have received the most recognition. Going back to the man-to-man war between Sam Huff, the New York Giants' middle linebacker, and Jimmy Brown, the Cleveland Browns' great fullback, the NFL has for years heralded the exploits of their linebackers. They are the sum and substance of the defense, whether you are in youth football or the Big Ten collegiate football league. Defenses are built around linebackers; they are the heart of it.

HOW TO CHOOSE LINEBACKERS

The offense has its quarterback and the defense has its linebacker. The things that the quarterback is expected to do for the offensive unit are the same things the linebacker is supposed to do for the defense. The first quality that must be reviewed is that of leadership. When things are going badly and the offense can't move the ball, the coach expects his quarterback to rally the team together for a maximum effort to turn the tide around for them. A good linebacker must do the same things when the defense is falling down on its job.

There is little doubt. that when players are aroused they often play way over their heads. Finding the right way to arouse them is the linebacker's task. Some teams want encouragement; others want to be screamed at. Whatever is necessary must be done. The emotional aspects of football are significant.

Many coaches find it wise to have their captains be both quarterbacks and linebackers because it becomes a natural extension of their leadership roles. To be a leader, you have to be respected and admired. This usually occurs when you are well liked by your teammates and when you are an outstanding football player.

Being a good player adds to your image as the leader of the team. If you fail to hold up your end, the team will feel that you are letting them down and you will lose some of the respect they have for you. For this reason, the coach's choice of a linebacker is very important and you have to understand what is expected of you if you go out for that position.

PHYSICAL REQUIREMENTS

A linebacker has to be big, strong, and tough. He does not have to be as big as the interior linemen because it would reduce his speed, but he does have to be of average size for his class of ball in order to withstand the stress placed on him and the position he plays. He must also be tall enough to be able to see what's happening in the offensive backfield when all the big linemen on both sides of the line of scrimmage start their attacks and counterattacks when the ball is snapped.

His agility must be well above average because so many of the things he is expected to do require him to react quickly, to control his legs and body as he rushes to the area that the running back is attacking. Agility will also help him avoid the blockers who come at him from all angles. On running plays, depending on the

The linebacker runs all the way to the sideline to make the tackle as a defensive back comes up to help.

direction in which the ball is going, he may be blocked from the front or from both sides. On sweeps it is not unheard of for him to be blocked from behind, inside the legal clip zone. Without quick feet and reflexes, he will spend most of his time on the ground rather than making the tackles that his position demands. His strength should be equal to that of anyone of his size so he can fight off the strong fire blocks that come at him play after play. Strength also provides stamina and the ability to hold up for the entire game. As important as a linebacker is to his team, any defender who folds in the second half will open the door to the opponent's offense and the game will probably be lost.

BUILDING STRENGTH FOR THE JOB

The best way to prepare for the linebacker position is to develop the strength of your entire body. You must work on your legs, your arms and shoulders, and your hands. Try to maximize your bench press ability and build up your torso to its fullest. When the big offensive linemen hurl their full weight and strength at you, you will be glad that you did all you could to build yourself up. Without it, you will be unable to hold your ground.

A full weight program is a necessity. This not only adds to your strength; it also makes you less prone to injury. Anyone who gets involved with as much contact as a linebacker does will end up with aches and pains or some disabling injury that will prevent you from playing.

AGILITY, QUICKNESS, AND SPEED

To develop these important physical attributes, a linebacker should do the same things that other players who also need these abilities must do. Frequent references have been made to jumping rope as a means of developing coordination. The linebackers need this as much, if not more, than anyone. It will give you the reaction capability to move into the thick of the action.

The running requirement as stated for running backs also applies to linebackers. They must be able to run to perform their pass coverage responsibilities and to pursue down the line of scrimmage to make a key tackle on the corner on an end sweep. Running must consist of sprints first and distance second. The forty-yard sprints that the running backs train with are ideal for the linebacker. Run a forty-yard dash and then coast or jog another forty yards. Start at one end of the field on the ten-yard line and sprint to the fifty and jog in at half speed to the other ten. Start with four ups and downs for one week and then add another up and down each week thereafter until you get to eight, and hold it there.

Quickness comes mainly through the use of drills. The tires, rope web, and plastic tubes requirement is also suited to the linebacker. They will give you the quick feet you must have. And the full-team agility drills that the coach will put you through will add to your quickness. Work on it and it will come.

STANCE, FOOTWORK, AND TECHNIQUES

The linebacker's stance is unique to the game of football. There is no other like it because no other position is faced with all the attack angles that face the linebacker. His stance must protect him from all these pitfalls to give him the time to see what the offense is doing. As he prepares for the snap of the ball, he must go into what is known as a *break down* position. This means that he must stand with his legs under his armpits, his knees flexed just enough to allow him to raise his weight forward on the balls of his feet. His stance requires him to put his inside foot about one foot farther away from the line of scrimmage than his outside foot. While in this semicrouched position he must raise his forearms until his fists are level to his chest as he girds himself for the offensive thrust.

When he sees the ball snapped, he must lean forward in anticipation of the charge of the blocker. At that moment, he must step forward and make his charge up from under the blocker's chest to stand him up and take his offensive charge away from him. He should then "chuck," or push aside, the blocker and proceed to an intersect point with the running back.

One of the most popular techniques that linebackers use, of course, is the stunt. A few examples were reviewed earlier, but there are others worth mentioning here (see diagram top right).

FOUR-MAN LINEBACKER STUNT

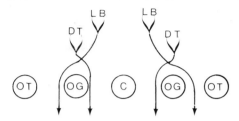

Linebackers practice their stances in pregame warm-up as teammates fire block into them.

Three linebackers lean forward to anticipate the move of the blockers coming at them on every play.

THREE-MAN LINEBACKER STUNT

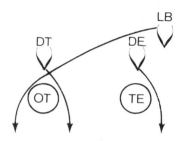

This is a four-man stunt. Both defensive tackles take an inside slant to converge on either side of the center and hope to make contact with the quarterback as he moves away from the center with the ball. At the same time, both linebackers take an outside approach and try to move quickly past the offensive guard and the offensive tackle. The accent must be on speed along with the strength and power that the linebacker has developed for moments like this. After penetrating the line of scrimmage, he must find the ball and get to it as fast as he can. This stunt may be reversed, with the defensive tackles going outside and the linebackers going inside.

Another favorite that always yielded good results is the three-man stunt that involves the defensive tackle, the defensive end, and the linebacker (see diagram at left). The idea behind many stunts is to disguise the fact that the linebacker is going in for a kill. In this one, both the defensive tackle and the defensive end go in to their left and the linebacker circles around behind them to go into the gap that the offensive tackle created when he tried to block the defensive tackle. Stunts are great when they work, but they can also backfire if you do them at the wrong time or if you do them poorly.

PASS COVERAGE RESPONSIBILITY

The linebacker is an important part of the pass coverage of the defense. His role can be that of occupying a place in the secondary, that of covering a man one on one, or even part of the pass rush designed to sack the quarterback or force him to throw off balance or sooner than he wants to. We have already reviewed the stunt as either an attack on a run or a pass. Let's look at the pass coverage responsibilities from a zone and from a man coverage (see diagram below).

In the four-linebacker defense of the 4-4-3, the short zone area is divided into four equal parts. Each of the linebackers, when he reads pass in the offensive backfield, must rush back and try

FOUR-MAN LINEBACKER ZONE

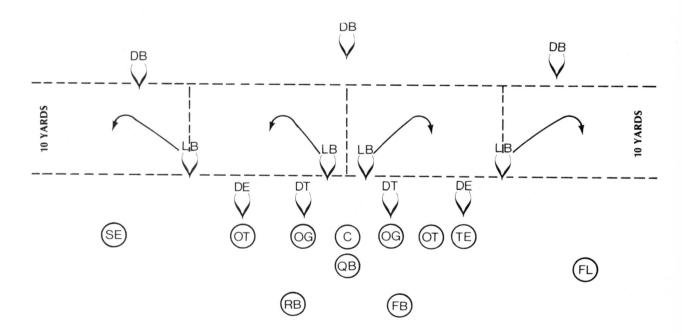

The three linebackers in this 5-3-3 defense will have to move quickly on this third down play to go to their hook zones if the quarterback shows pass as he leaves the center.

to get himself in the middle of his assigned area. When he follows the movement of backs or receivers coming into his zone, he must go to them and stay with them until the pass is thrown or until the player leaves the zone.

In the three-linebacker formation of the 5-3-3 or in the rotation out of a 5-4-2 that ends up with three linebackers in the short zone and a

three-deep arrangement in the deep zone, the linebackers each have to cover one third of the field, sideline to sideline (see diagram below).

In either or any case, zone coverage requires that attention be paid to the seams between the zones where the receivers try to be when the quarterback throws the ball to them. Therefore, linebackers and safeties must not only be aware

THREE-MAN LINEBACKER ZONE

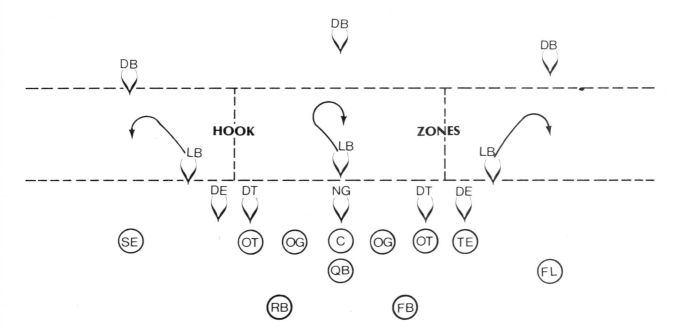

LINEBACKER MAN-TO-MAN COVERAGE ASSIGNMENTS

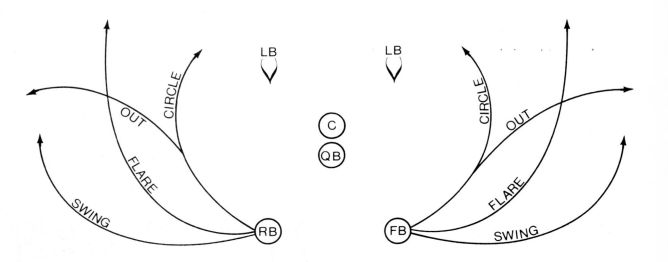

of the receivers in their zones, they must ease themselves out of the center of their zones if there are no other receivers to threaten them and try to cover the seams whenever they can.

In man-to-man coverage, the linebacker usually is responsible for the closest back to his side of the field, wherever he goes. Regardless of which type of pattern his back runs, the linebacker must stay with him (see diagram above). The most difficult parts of this assignment are having the speed to stay with him, which is another reason why linebackers have to be fast, and avoiding getting trapped in the crowd at the line of scrimmage. The rule for linebackers is that when you read pass, drop back to your zone quickly or pick up the location of your man and get to his side.

DEFENSIVE QUARTERBACK ROLE

The linebacker calls the defenses in the defensive huddle. He may be permitted to do this according to his own judgment or he may get signals from the bench on each play. Because of the growth in strategy for defensive tactics, the coaches are increasingly assuming full responsibility for calling plays for both offense and defense. However, as in the case of the offense, the coach has to develop a defensive game plan

based on the scouting reports and the strengths and weaknesses of his team and the opponent's team. The linebacker must know and understand what the coach wants to do. He must also be well aware of what the opponents do well and when they are likely to do them. For example, a stunt called on third down that sends in both linebackers against a team that likes to throw a quick pass over the middle to a big tight end is not a wise move.

The linebacker's job is to implement the defensive plan on the field. In addition to calling the formation, he may want to remind his teammates about something that may be coming at them. He must also encourage the players who are angry with themselves for an earlier mistake, or he may want to reprimand someone for a bad judgment that gave the offense an advantage.

Perhaps more than anything else, he must be an inspiration to his team. You may do this simply by doing it all on the field; the other players are motivated by your example to do the same. Or you may be a "holler" guy who gives them the spark to play hard by cheering them up and by drumming up enthusiasm over every good thing that anyone does. You have to make the defense give every ounce of energy and instill in them the spirit and pride they need to be a good unit.

TRAINING TO DEVELOP SKILLS

To summarize, the really important skills that a linebacker must have are strength, speed, and technique. More than enough has been said about strength and speed and how you go about developing your body to make you as good as you can be. The linebacker techniques that you must improve on are tackling, pass coverage, pursuit actions, and handling of the offensive blockers on the line of scrimmage.

When you assume your stance about one yard off the line of scrimmage in your break-down stance, you must be able to go in every direction, know where and why you are going there, and then must do your thing when you get there. The thing you have to do most is to securely tackle the ball carrier. Linebackers make more tackles than anyone on the team as a general rule. The team cannot afford to have missed tackles at this position because they will often lead to long runs and touchdowns. The only players between the linebackers and the goal line are the safeties. To state that linebackers must do all the tackling drills with eagerness and good style is putting it mildly.

The linebacker (number 45) hits the ball carrier with such force that he takes him clear off the ground with a crunching and jarring tackle.

Pass coverage can be improved as the daily skeleton drills are performed under the coach's direction. These drills call for the omission of guards and tackles, both offensive and defensive, to allow the offense to throw against the defenders who have pass coverage duties. Linebackers play an important role in this drill since they pick up receivers running short zone patterns or they pick up backs coming at them out of the backfield.

As to the handling of the blockers coming off the line of scrimmage, it is possible to work on this in preseason by getting an offensive lineman to work with you as he practices his blocking and you work on fighting off his block. Either by using shoulder pads and helmets or by using dummies, your skill can be improved. Remember, linebackers have to be able to do it all.

15 | Defensive Backs—The Umbrella Crew

HOW TO CHOOSE DEFENSIVE BACKS

Defensive backs are the players who play safety and cornerback. They play very important positions because they must protect against the pass and they must make tackles when the linemen and linebackers fail to do so. In most defensive formations there are either three or four defensive backs. In the three-back setup, they are usually called left safety, middle safety, and right safety; and they are arranged in the manner shown in the diagram, top of page 132.

In the four-back arrangement, they are often called the left cornerback, left safety, right safety, and right cornerback; and they are lined up as shown in the diagram, bottom of page 132. (Note that left and right safety are also known as strong and free safety.)

Defensive backs are selected from the pool of players that go out for the offensive positions of quarterback, running back, and wide receiver. In

the selection process, the coach will measure speed, quickness, and coordination and compare them in abilities like catching the ball, running with the ball, and so on. But the bottom line is the important ability to tackle because, if there is one talent a defensive back must have, it is to make sure tackles.

As is true of linebackers, the defensive backs must be mentally suited to the position. They must have a great deal of pride in their ability because their activities are usually out in the open for everyone to see. If they allow a pass completion or miss a tackle, everyone at the game will be able to see it. Players whose personalities can't recover from situations like this should not be playing this position. They must also be tough-minded, which means that they will have to withstand the hard play and contact that they will see a great deal of in the secondary.

THREE-MAN SAFETY ZONE

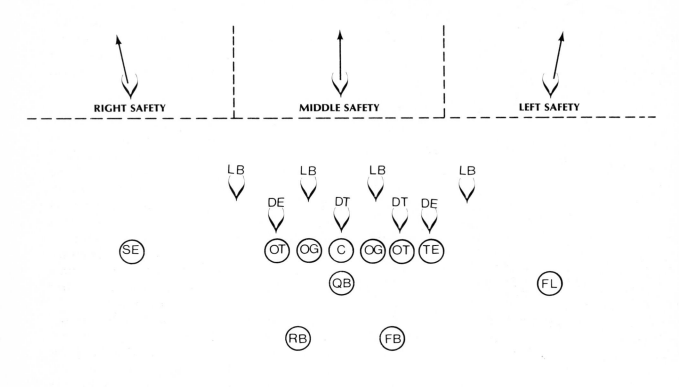

FOUR-MAN SAFETY ZONE

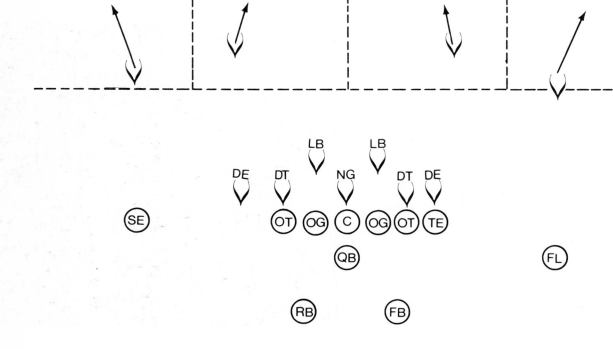

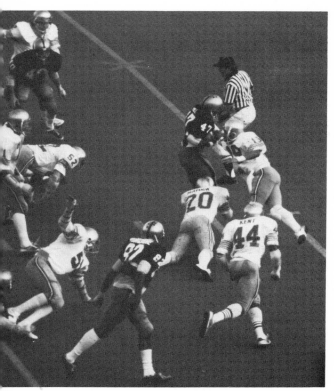

Two defensive backs come up to make the tackle on the ball carrier to stop a touchdown on the five-yard line.

PHYSICAL REQUIREMENTS

When reviewing the pool of players in order to make a judgment as to which ones should play defensive back, you will note that the fastest runners will usually be running backs and defensive backs; the bulkier ones will be running backs and the slimmer ones will be defensive backs.

Slimness can be tolerated in these positions because these players are seldom hit. They do the hitting and, if they tackle properly, they don't need all the bulk that players in most other positions must have. Speed, coupled with slimness, makes it possible for them to get places quickly to cover the fast wide receivers on pass plays and to rush up toward the line of scrimmage to tackle on running plays.

Being slim does not mean that you can't be strong. In fact, it makes strength even more important because, without the weight behind you, your strength must make it possible for you to hit and sting people when you tackle. Review the physical requirements for offensive linemen

and understand that you can do wonders with your body if you follow similar guidelines. Your concentration must be focused on upper body development and the strengthening and buildup of your legs. Leg buildup will increase your speed and you will never have too much of that.

DEVELOPING YOUR SPEED

Without above-average speed, a player cannot successfully fill the duties of a defensive back. In fact, the defensive back should think of himself as a member of the track team and do all the things that a sprinter does to improve his speed. The only thing that doesn't apply is the starting stance of a sprinter; but the defensive back must be poised for takeoff at the start of each play. His reaction ability is vital to his arrival on the scene where the ball is. And keeping up with a speedy wide receiver racing down the sideline will require all the speed he can muster.

Concentration must be placed on the development of the thighs. This can be done in a number of ways. An old but good technique is the upside-down bicycle ride. Get on your back, raise your legs and hips, holding them by your hands in a propped-up position, and extend your feet toward the sky. Then begin to pump

From the outside, two defensive backs are on a "safety fire," a stunt in which they rush the passer, trying to use their speed to get to him before he has time to throw.

your legs as though you were riding a bicycle. The entire weight of your legs will be supported by your thigh muscles and, as they pump away, you'll be giving them a full workout.

Another way to build up the thighs is to jump rope with more emphasis on getting your body as high off the ground as you can. Jumping up and down forces your thighs to generate strength. If you don't have a rope, a simple jumping exercise can be used. Pretend you are a basketball player and you are trying to jump up to stuff the ball. Standing in one place and jumping up and down will strengthen your thigh and other leg muscles.

Mix some or all of the above with your regular sprint drills. Once again, we recommend the forty-yard sprints followed by a forty-yard jog to recover your breath. The more forty-yard sprints you do over a period of weeks and months, the more the thigh muscles will develop and the faster you will be able to run. When you sprint, be aware of the pumping of your arms and be sure to keep them under tight control because they control the speed and rhythm of your running ability.

STANCE, FOOTWORK, AND TECHNIQUES

The defensive back's stance varies depending on where he is playing. If he is playing a middle safety (or strong safety, as it is sometimes called) about seven to ten yards off the line of scrimmage per his coach's direction, he should stand in an almost upright position with his body leaning slightly toward the line of scrimmage, bent at the waist, and his eyes fixed on the offensive man he is using as his key. One foot is about a foot behind the other, shoulder width apart, and the arms hang loosely, waiting for the play to begin. When the ball is snapped, the first step is taken backward on the back foot.

This is intended to keep the defensive back from rushing up to the line of scrimmage too quickly and being fooled by a pass. While taking the first step, the defensive back must read his key. If it is the tight end and the tight end shows block, then the defensive back may come forward as he reads the flow of the play. If the tight end releases downfield, the defensive back must freeze, anticipate a pass, and try to read what the offense is doing while he follows the path of the defensive end coming downfield.

On a third down and eleven play, all defensive backs are poised ready to come out of their stances to cover the receivers coming downfield for the long pass.

The defensive back plays up tight on the flanker to bump and run with him to break up the timing of the play.

If the defensive back is a cornerback and is split out toward the sideline in a man-on-man coverage on a wide receiver, and his coach wants him to play up on the wide receiver to bump and run with him, the defensive back's stance is a crouched position, on an angle to the line of scrimmage with his back toward the middle of the field. As he leans forward, eyes fixed on his man, he must be prepared to come up the one or two steps between him and the wide receiver to give him a forearm shiver into the chest. This bump is intended to break his stride as he comes off the line of scrimmage, disrupt the timing of the play, and allow the defensive back to recover and run with the wide receiver as they both head downfield.

This is a very difficult and dangerous technique to use and only the most skilled of defensive backs should try it. If the wide receiver turns to the sideline, the defensive back must turn quickly with him or the quarterback will deliver the ball and the pass will be completed. When the wide receiver races downfield on a fly pattern, the defensive back's back will be facing the quarterback and, therefore, he will not be able to see the ball. When he sees the wide receiver looking for the ball prior to catching it, the defensive back must also turn and try to knock it

down or intercept it. As you can see, it is a difficult way to cover, but a good way if you have the skill and training to do it.

A cornerback with zone coverage usually means that he will be covering the flat area. In this role, he is just like an outside linebacker and must take a position two to three yards off the line of scrimmage and about three yards outside the tight end (see diagram on page 136). He may take a linebacker's stance, turn diagonally to the line of scrimmage with his back toward the sideline, and read his key as he awaits the snap of the ball. If the ball is run in his direction, he must come across the line of scrimmage, assume a defensive end stance with one leg back, arms hanging down to ward off any blocks and shoulders parallel with the line of scrimmage. His job is to keep the sweep from turning upfield and to force the running back to run to the sideline.

PASS COVERAGE RESPONSIBILITIES

Pass coverage that involves the zone defense requires the defensive back to know his area of responsibility and to defend it thoroughly. The full 4-3 deep formation zone assignments are shown in the diagram on page 136. In the deep

ZONE 4-3 DEEP FORMATION

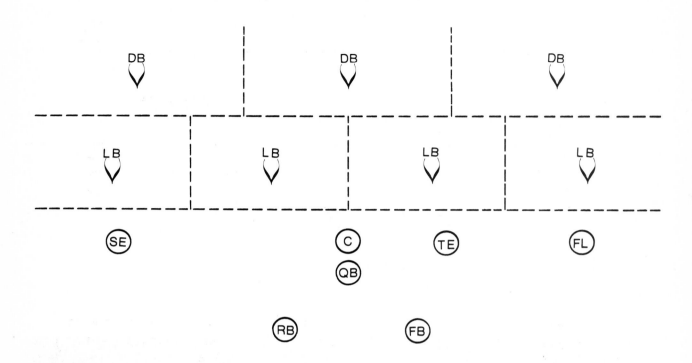

secondary, the defensive backs must cover any receiver who comes into their zone all the way back to the goal line. Defensive backs must never let a wide receiver get behind them in a deep zone. If no one goes into their zone, they must then read the offensive flow, look for receivers in adjacent zones, and follow the flight of the ball until it leads them to the receiver.

In the up zones, their coverage must include the area from their flat back to the front of the deep zone. Sometimes knowing where the up zone ends and the deep zone begins is a problem. Most coaches say that about ten yards is the maximum depth of the up zone and do not expect their defensive backs to cover deeper than that. Any variations must be worked out with the deep defensive backs and the coaching staff.

In man-to-man coverage in the 4-3 deep formation, the players that are usually covered by defensive backs are indicated in the diagram on page 137.

When there are twin wide receivers to one side, the wide man is covered by the wide defensive back who should play him inside out. This means that the defensive back would be closer to

the middle of the field to take away any inside slant pattern that might be run, while the sideline would help protect against any outside route. This is proper coverage technique for any defensive back covering any wide receiver near the sideline. Because both wide receivers in a twin set could go on deep routes, the two defensive backs must cover them, but the outside linebacker may have flat zone responsibility. It is not uncommon for a coach to use a man-to-man defense coupled with a zone defense. The other linebackers would all have up-zone duty and the deep defensive backs would cover the other receivers on a man-to-man basis.

READING THE OFFENSIVE FORMATION

Because a defensive back's coverage assignment depends on the formations that the offense may use, and the decision of the coach as to whether he wants zone, man or a combination of both, when the offense breaks out of its huddle the defensive back must quickly read and understand what their formation is and what he must do to cover it. This may require him to relocate to a different place on the field, even

MAN 4-3 DEEP FORMATION

MAN-TO-MAN DEFENSIVE BACK COVERAGE

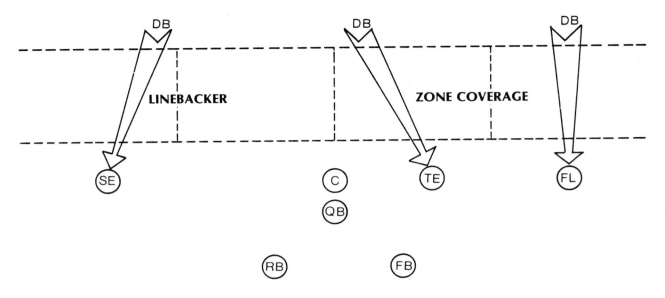

LINEBACKER   **ZONE COVERAGE**

Two defensive backs line up opposite twin receivers to their side of the field on man-to-man coverage.

flipping to the other side of the field if the coach wants him to cover a particular wide receiver.

In order to be sure that he is in the right place, he must look for the tight end as he comes out of the huddle. This is true because many tight ends flip from one side of the center to the other, based on the formation the quarterback has called and the location of the wide receivers. After locating the tight end, the defensive back must then look for the placement of the wide receivers and of any running backs who may be placed in a slot or a wing position. In man-to-man coverage the rule usually is that the outside defensive back in a deep set covers the widest receiver and the second receiver in from the sideline is covered by the next defensive back in. If there is any doubt, they must talk to each other and decide which one each of them will cover. There cannot be any confusion about who covers which wide receiver or disaster could strike.

Another problem for the defensive backs is the use of a man in motion. This complicates the coverage because it almost always forces the defense to rotate toward the motion and changes some defensive backs' responsibilities. Look at the diagram below and see what the defense looks like before and after the man in motion takes off on his run toward the sideline.

Defensive back (number 23) finds the tight end as he comes out of the huddle and keys (reacts to) him when the play starts.

The defense was up to its right, which means that it was rotating its cornerbacks and safeties to the strong side of the offense because they had twins to the offense's left. When the slot wide receiver starts in motion, the defense then has to go up left because the strength of the offense has

MAN-IN-MOTION

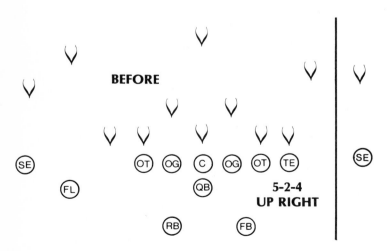

MAN-IN-MOTION REACTION

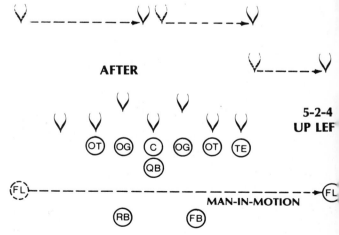

As the flanker starts in motion, the defensive backs must rotate toward the motion and change their coverage.

Defensive back (number 11) reaches out and makes a key interception to stop an offensive drive.

shifted from one side of the field to the other. Once again, it's a matter of matching strength with strength.

TRAINING TO DEVELOP SKILLS

One of the important skills for the defensive back is the ability to catch the football. He should spend many hours of his time trying to improve his catching ability in much the same manner as the wide receiver. Review chapter 7 to understand how to develop your catching talent and then practice it frequently both preseason and during the season.

There are some pass catching–reaction drills that are popular among defensive coaches. One of them is called the tip drill. In this activity the defensive backs are lined up about ten yards apart and the ball is thrown to the front man, who tries to tip it up in the air to give the back man a chance to catch it (see diagram, top of page 140). This is intended to simulate a game condition in which a pass may be overthrown by a quarterback and it deflects off the receiver's hands into the hands of the defensive back in the deep coverage area. This is a good way to learn

TIP DRILL

BACK LINE

DEFENSIVE BACKS

FRONT LINE

how to handle a ball, especially because it is rotating wildly and is not a perfect spiral.

Another good drill is really a man-to-man coverage drill (see diagram at bottom right), in which a defensive back lines up either in a five- to seven-yard deep set or in a bump and run set and tries to cover the pass routes that the wide receiver tells the quarterback he's going to run. In one part of this drill the quarterback tries to complete the pass, but in another part he throws the ball high in the air to give them both a chance to catch it. This represents the battle for a ball that the defensive back will have in his attempt to intercept or knock down the pass.

Running backward is another excellent drill for the defensive back. This is important to him because there are many occasions when he must backpedal in his coverage. The moves of a wide receiver are often done well enough to fool a defensive back and, if he isn't capable of fully controlling his body as he turns around, he may slip or trip and the wide receiver will be wide open when the ball arrives. This is one of the best coordination drills for every football player, and the defensive back must be the best player at it, for his footwork is so very vital to his success.

MAN-TO-MAN COVERAGE DRILL

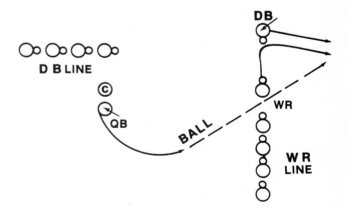

16 | Tackling Skills and Techniques— Stopping the Runner

TACKLING TECHNIQUES MADE EASY

Football players constantly hear that football is a game of blocking and tackling. Of the two, we have already pointed out that blocking is perhaps more difficult because it is not an instinctive reaction, as is tackling. When you see youngsters under age ten playing in a backyard, some of them make almost perfect tackles, even before anyone showed them how. On the other hand, you can often see college linemen, after years and years of training, still performing their blocks incorrectly.

Even though tackling may be a natural reaction, there are ways to do it right and there are more ways to do it wrong. In the early days of football, coaches told their players to aim all their tackles at the knees of the ball carrier. The reasoning was good. If you take the legs out from under a ball carrier, he will go down. As years went by and running backs became more skilled at avoiding tackles by juking, sharp fakes and cuts, straight arming, etc., tacklers began missing ball carriers far more often than ever before.

The old football axiom that if the offense does something, the defense must counteract it, came true again because the style of tackling started to change. Coaches realized that when the tackler dove for the knees of the running back, not only could the running back fake the runner and cause him to miss his legs, but the tackler was now on the ground and out of the play. Further, while the running back's legs were going one way, his upper body was shifting to go another way and the tackle would be missed. This forced a change in logic. In order to make tackling more successful, the running back himself had to be tackled, not just his legs. The running back's body is a much bigger target to aim for and, by tackling his body and using the full strength of the tackler, the running back can be stopped and brought down. In addition, by aiming for the body, the tackler is not on a nose dive for the turf; and if he missed the running back, he would still be in an upright position to stay on his feet and continue his pursuit.

How to Execute Various Tackling Methods

There are different ways of tackling, depending on the situation, the position the defender plays, and the location on the field. We'll take the most common one and the one that best expresses the change in tackling techniques.

Interior linemen and linebackers are most often faced with the task of tackling a running back in a crowd somewhere near the line of scrimmage. When the defensive tackle, nose guard, or defensive end makes his initial charge into his opponent, his first objective is to get past his blocker; the next is to find the ball and make the tackle. These players must stay on their feet in a forward leaning position, and usually that is what their stance looks like when they encounter the running back trying to run the ball through a hole that may no longer exist because they avoided the block. The one-on-one match-up begins.

The target of the tackler is now the area between the belt and the chest of the running back. He should try to stick his head into the side of the running back's chest that is closest to him so that his shoulder hits the running back squarely in the soft spot just below the chest. This is the center of the running back's strength. He is running with a forward lean and is attempting to lower his shoulder into the oncoming tacklers to use his momentum and strength to break the tackle. If he were tackled at the ankles, his momentum would carry him a few yards downfield; if his balance was really good, he might even recover and continue to gain valuable yardage.

The best way to stop him from gaining ground is to stop his forward progress. This can be done only by stopping his body because it is the source of his strength and momentum. This is the moment when the defensive lineman's

LINEBACKER REACTION

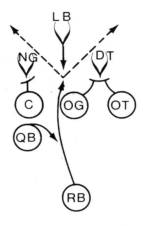

strength is pitted against the running back's power. All the weight training comes into play and the success of the defender often is directly related to how strong he is when the running back runs into him.

The situation for the linebacker is very similar. On many occasions the blockers are successful in taking the defensive linemen out of the hole but fail to get the linebacker. When the hole opens up, the running back suddenly sees a linebacker directly in the way of his run to daylight. By now the running back has picked up momentum, is running a little faster, and has a choice of going right through the linebacker or veering off to one side or the other of him (see diagram above). It is for this reason that the linebacker must step up into the hole when he sees the running back coming toward him. This technique not only allows him to pick up some of his momentum; it also tends to plug the hole to give the running back less room to veer off to his left or right.

The linebacker's target is the same as the lineman's. From his crouched stance, he must come up under the running back's shoulder and deliver a blow with his shoulder to drive the running back up and back. At the moment his shoulder hits, his arms must come swinging around the running back's body to clamp on it and try to raise the running back off the ground. While all this is going on, the linebacker's head should be pulled into his neck and shoulders and raised slightly to permit his eyes to have a

An open-field tackle is made by the defensive back (number 20) to keep the ball carrier from making a long run.

As the running back heads downfield, the defensive back (number 12) takes a sharper angle of pursuit to tackle him.

full view of where the running back is or is going. It is very important that the tackle be made squarely in the middle of the running back's body or it will increase the chances of missing the tackle. Remember that the running back is taught to spin and twist when he is being tackled and a glancing tackle will not ensure success. The linebacker must make a sure tackle because he is the gateway to daylight.

The defensive backs are the last line of de-

fense. If they miss a tackle, the offense may get a touchdown. Their tackling methods must be more certain than anyone else's. When they encounter the running back, he is often cranking up his full speed and power because he is past the line of scrimmage and is ready to show his skill as a running back. The defensive back is frequently faced with a one-on-one situation complicated by some downfield blockers who often only have to get in the defensive back's way to give the running back the room he needs to get beyond him. Therefore, the defensive back must quickly evaluate his situation and take the course of action that gives him the best chance of making the tackle, even though, in some cases, it may mean much farther down the field. This means he must consider the angle of his pursuit, taking into consideration where the blockers are and where the running back is heading. He must get near the ball.

When this effort is successful, his next task is to try to get as close to the running back as possible. To do this he must try to determine whether or not his speed is greater than the running back's. If he feels he can gain on him, he would be better off waiting until he gets closer to guarantee the tackle than to take a chance with a diving tackle from behind. Once he gets close enough, he should aim for the running back's shoulders and try to get his arms around the running back's neck and shoulders to drag him down. The hips and legs must not be considered because it is much easier to slip off them than off the shoulders.

Of course, if there is no other choice, a diving lunge at any part of the running back's body may have to be made, but this must be your last resort. If you are near the sideline, you may be able to throw your body into his, even if it is a glancing blow, to force him out of bounds. Any attempt is better than simply letting a running back run away from you, which is something that is often seen because a defensive back waited too long to make a good judgment.

At one time or another, any defensive player may be faced with the need for a quick decision as to which way to attempt his tackle. Be sure to look around you and be aware of where your teammates are. A defensive end, for example, may try a diving tackle if it is the best shot he has at a running back on a sweep because he knows that his cornerback is just outside of him and can make a better attempt if the defensive end misses. The same situation often applies to a defensive back in an open field, where his tackle may be questionable but he knows that a teammate is right behind him.

TACKLING THE BIG RUNNING BACK

Another part of the decision that a defender must make as he considers the tackling problem that is about to confront him is the size and strength of the running back who is carrying the ball. Information about each running back is usually part of the scouting report and members of the defensive unit are expected to know what to expect before they even set foot on the field for the game. The best information comes after you've made a tackle or two because you may find out what it takes to bring a certain running back down. Make a judgment for future reference.

If the offense has a big powerful running back whose ability is based on brute strength and not on speed and elusiveness, a different tackling problem confronts the defense. The first conclusion that should be reached is that he most likely will not be taken down by one man. Even though there may be a high opinion of the defense's ability, it is far wiser to decide that, whenever this kind of running back is carrying

the ball, he should be tackled by as many people as possible.

As a general rule, big backs are tackled easier from above. If you try to tackle their legs, their leg strength and ability to shiver with their free forearm will most likely break your tackle and they will get loose for more yardage. Linemen and linebackers must make a stronger effort to straighten a big back up to take away his shoulder power and to expose more of his body to the other defenders. Once he has been hit and is slowed down, it may be possible to take his legs out by driving through his knees. This should not be the first hit. If you are approaching him from the side, go for his shoulders and ride him like a bronco rider bringing down his animal. Even wrap your legs around him, if you can, as an added means of getting him down.

SACKING THE QUARTERBACK

Making a tackle on a quarterback as a running back is no different from tackling any other ball carrier. But, when the quarterback goes back to throw the ball, a definite approach should be followed. One of the most difficult problems for a quarterback is the ability to see the receivers running their pass routes. This problem is increased by the size and height of both the offensive and defensive linemen. The offensive linemen try to stay low as they perform their pass blocks because it enables them to

The big running back draws a crowd as the defense makes a gang tackle on him to help wear him down.

recover from their blocking thrusts. However, the defensive linemen usually come in high as they attempt to make their pass rush past the blockers to get at the quarterback. Coming in high with arms flailing gives the quarterback reduced visibility and causes him to move slightly to his left or right as he attempts to find the guys running their routes.

When the pass rushers are swimming and pushing the blockers' shoulders and heads to throw them off balance, they must follow the movements of the quarterback and adjust their charge to his movements. At the same time they should extend their arms toward the sky to make it even more difficult for him to see. From this continuous action, the defenders should try to tackle the quarterback around the neck as it will best interfere with his throwing arm. It is common to see a defender draped around the quarterback's hips while he still manages to throw the ball to a nearby running back to avoid a loss. Whenever the quarterback's arm is deflected with this tackling approach, there's a good chance of an interception or a fumble. In either case, the defense will be doing its job.

PURSUIT TECHNIQUES

Pursuit is defined as the action a defender takes to get to a position on the field where he may be able to tackle the ball carrier. Sometimes

a defensive man only has to look up to find the ball, and his pursuit is over. On the other hand, the ball often goes to the other side of the field from where you are playing and your angle of pursuit may be a long and difficult one to perform. Every member of the defense should be involved in pursuit on every play of a game.

The best defensive units are those that have as many people as possible getting to the ball or in on the tackle. This means that everyone is aware of what is going on and is reacting to the flow of the play. If someone misses a tackle, there are more players around to make the tackle and prevent the offense from making more yardage. But knowing where to go, after a play has begun, is not always a simple matter.

First of all, it is important to find the ball. Sometimes the deception in the offensive backfield makes it difficult to react quickly. In fact, you shouldn't react until you are sure you know where the ball really is. Defenders who react too soon often allow reverses, draws, and counters to be successful because they chased a rainbow instead of finding out for certain where the ball was. After finding the ball, the defender must make a quick judgment of where is it likely to go and what his best chances are of getting in on the action. When he concludes that it may be possible to get to the ball carrier, he must then decide on which course is the best for him to follow. This determines his angle of pursuit,

ANGLE OF PURSUIT

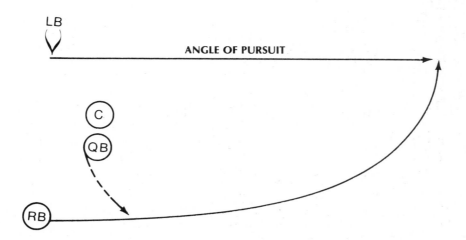

and if his judgment is good, he should be able to get to the ball somewhere on the field.

There are a few rules to follow in taking your angle of pursuit. First, you must anticipate the distance you will have to travel to get to where the ball will be when you get there. Second, you should adjust your angle if you see that another member of your team is taking the same angle that you are (see diagram on page 145). The running back is heading around his right end and, at the speed at which he can run, you have to figure that he will be downfield somewhere by the time you can get there. Of course, someone may tackle him before he gets there, but that's good. Even though your effort may be in vain if he is tackled, you must plan on the worst situation, which would be that he is still going when you get to the intersect point and you could get to him.

If one of your teammates is ahead of you and heading for the same intersect point, you won't be able to make the tackle anyway because he will be in your way. Therefore, you should adjust your angle to a point farther downfield just in case your teammate doesn't get him. "Never follow the same-colored jersey" is an old expression that will give you an easy rule to remember. And "never run to where the running back is; run to where he will be" is the other rule to remember. Make pursuit a habit in your defensive play because it often makes the difference between success and failure.

PRACTICE AND TRAINING TO IMPROVE

A variety of things can be done to improve the tackling skills of every defensive player. Some of them involve drills and others involve equipment. Let's evaluate the use of equipment first because some of the equipment must be used for the drills. Depending on the level of ball you are playing, you may or may not have access to some of the really good training devices that are now available.

Probably the most common piece of equipment that is available is the tackling sled. This is a heavy metal device that has a cylinder dummy attached to a spring steel plate on a heavily weighted pontoonlike sled. When the dummy is tackled the sled may be pushed over

A sure tackle is made on the running back by the defensive back as his teammates rush in on their angles of pursuit to help.

the turf, and its weight offers good resistance to the tackler. The coach will probably use this sled every day in his practice plan and give every member of the defensive unit an opportunity to tackle it (see diagram at top of page 147).

While the tacklers take turns performing their tackling techniques, the coach stands alongside and makes any corrective comments that are necessary. He may point out that a tackler hit the dummy too low or high, or that there was no force behind the tackle, or that there was too little follow-through to provide the drive necessary to bring a running back down. Often, the players start to lunge or dive from too far away, which, in a live tackling situation, may cause a tackle to be missed. There are many ways of tackling incorrectly, but the above are most of the common errors that are made. Your coach will give you a good critique of your performance.

Another tackling device is a hanging tackling

TACKLING SLED DRILL

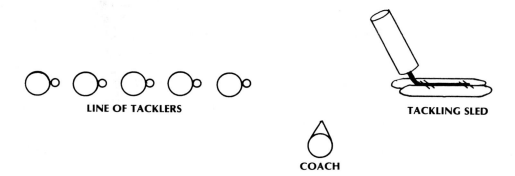

dummy. This piece of equipment is usually hung from an overhead rig with a rope or cable that has a weight attached to it to offer a force to be overcome by the tackler. Sometimes the dummy is in the actual form of a body; others are cylindrical dummies like the one on the tackling sled. In either case, they offer the tackler an excellent tool to use to practice their tackling technique and to improve their skills. Both of these devices may be used either before or after practice if you feel you need more work on your tackling. Don't be ashamed to go at it yourself because, in the final analysis, you will be the one to get the most benefit out of it.

There are also a few really good tackling drills in which all players should participate. The first of them provides a real, live tackling situation in which a reaction and a tackle are needed in a hurry. We have always called it the scramble drill (see diagram below). Two lines of players are required. One line is the ball carrying group and the other is the tackling group. The coach may elect to use only running backs for the ball carriers, but if they are busy elsewhere on the

practice field, the coach may use other defensive men to carry the ball and to tackle.

Both players lie on their backs with their heads pointing at each other. The two dummies on the side establish the area for the contest. When the coach blows the whistle, they both scramble to their feet; the ball carrier tries to get past the tackler while the tackler tries to hold him to no gain. The dummies represent the line of scrimmage. This drill provides the coach with an excellent evaluation of each defensive player and repeated use of it usually results in improved tackling ability.

The other drill that stresses open-field tackling in a live situation is the down-the-line drill. Once again, the coach may elect to use running backs to help improve their skills as ball carriers. The typical arrangement for this drill is seen in the diagram on page 148. With two lines, one of tacklers and one of ball carriers, a one-on-one situation calls for the ball carrier to run down the line and make the decision by himself as to which two dummies he will run between to turn upfield to get past the tackler. The tackler must

SCRAMBLE DRILL

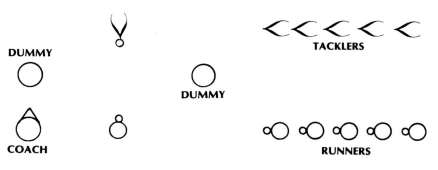

DOWN-THE-LINE DRILL

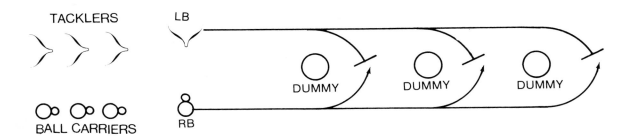

pursue down the line and, when he sees the ball coming toward him, he must turn, get his shoulders square to the line of scrimmage, and deliver his tackling blow into the ball carrier's midsection. There is more momentum in this drill than the other one, but both represent real tackling situations.

Your tackling ability, or lack of it, will be evident in both of these drills. As you improve, you will find that all the skill development you have accomplished with your weight training program, your running, agility and quickness improvements will come to the fore as you show your coach what you are able to do. If there are areas still in need of improvement, your coach will advise you and help you find the right way to improve. You must provide the interest and energy along with your dedication.

17 | Getting the Most Out of Practice

Football is a sport that requires a good deal of individual energy and dedication, not only during the season, but also in the preseason. Pre–high school youngsters often play all the sports that are available in their neighborhool and/or school athletic programs. By the time they get to high school, young boys tend to specialize in only a few sports, giving up on others that they don't enjoy as much or aren't very good in. In either case, boys who enjoy athletics find a way to stay active physically all year long and really never get out of condition.

However, just staying active is not really enough for those who wish to concentrate on football as their main athletic interest. In each chapter we have covered many of the skills that must be developed and improved in order to excel in football. Many of these skills can be improved on a year-round program, particularly during the months that football isn't played. Whether you call it preseason for the things you do before the season starts or postseason for the things you do after the football season ends, there are things to be done.

Let's start with postseason activities. A long and hard season has ended and the year-end holiday season rolls around. It is wise to take a brief vacation from football and its demands and give yourself time to unwind and to review the results of the past season. Evaluate the things you did and break them down into three categories. First, identify the skills with which you are satisfied. These are things that may be improved on as you grow older but, for now, you think you're doing them as well as you can. Next, review the skills that were only average, that you know you can improve but that are not as bad as things that you really *must* improve. They are the third category in which you can really identify some skills that are below average, perhaps things that your coach told you had to be improved. Often, it may be something that only you know you are deficient in; the coach or your teammates may not be aware of it at all. Your own strength may fall into this category because it is very hard to tell whether or not a player really has enough strength.

Once you have established these priorities, plan how you are going to improve on the bad ones first and the average ones next. Let's continue with the assumption that strength is an area in which you really feel inadequate. In conjunction with your coach or your school's physical education teacher, establish a set of goals for yourself and develop a plan for achieving the goals. Perhaps you can only bench press 100 pounds. What do your advisors think your target should be for the end of each month, for the next five months? How much additional weight should you add each week to make your month-ending targets? These questions must be answered based on your height, weight, and body structure. A wide variety of strength-oriented objectives can be met. These include your legs, feet, arms, shoulders, etc.

For example, there are targets for repetitions that can be set for things like lateral raises for your arms, toe raises for your feet, shoulder shrugs for your shoulders, alternate curls for your arms, and triceps curls for your arms. There are also weight targets for the military press for your body, hack lift (behind your back) for your entire torso, squats with the weight bar across your shoulders for your body's strength, and power clean for your weight and coordination development. These are only a few of the various things that you can do to make your body measure up to what your football position will require.

Of course, another off-season program must be one to increase your speed. This must be recognized as a long-term project and not one that can be accomplished in only a couple of weeks. If you keep in mind that running is probably the best overall exercise you can do, the speed aspect of it must be only one of the important benefits. In the months of January,

February, and March, the basic off-season program should include a body building program and a running program. They can be done on alternate days or combined to be done on the same day. However, lifting while being overtired from running is not a good idea, so schedule them as far apart as possible or do them on alternate days. Your running should be mostly distance running, which will build up your leg muscles. On at least three days of the week, you should run forty-yard sprints from your position's stance. Be sure to have yourself timed to permit evaluation of progress.

In all of these activities, it is best to arrange to have some of your teammates participate. You may even be able to set up some form of competition with them to make the daily and weekly sessions more interesting. Another advantage is that they will be able to point out things they see that may need correction. Certainly it will be another way to develop the unity that all teammates must have if their team is going to be a close-knit one in which everyone cooperates with each other and the coaching staff.

As the season nears, perhaps a month before the start of official practices, you must also begin to increase the pace of your activities. This does not apply to your weight program because that must be a gradual, consistent regimen. But your running should include more sprints and greater emphasis on the running techniques you expect to use during the season. If you are a running back, you should try to run zigzag courses through or around tires and pylons. Work on your fakes and sharp cuts. If you are a wide receiver, run your pass routes and get them down pat. Of course, it is practical for the quarterbacks, wide receivers, and running backs to form a group to work out together, including some of the defensive backs to give them and the wide receivers a chance to work together.

Interior linemen should also gather together to work on their techniques, including their stances, pass rush, etc., versus the blocking techniques of their offensive counterparts.

The specialty players who punt, kick, and center the ball, including holders for place kicks and returners for punts and kickoffs, should also get together for combined practices.

SEASONAL PRACTICE SESSIONS

Each coach has his own ideas as to how to use practice time during the season. In general, sessions will include running, calisthenics, drills, blocking and tackling activities, special team's activities, and offensive and defensive team workouts. Deciding how much time to devote to each activity often depends on the number of assistant coaches on the staff. For example, if there are enough coaches to go around, an offensive coordinator could be working with the backs and an offensive line coach with the linemen. There might be another coach with the defensive secondary and a fourth with the defensive linemen.

Regardless of the number of coaches, every activity must be done efficiently and done thoroughly to get maximum benefit out of it. For the player, the only thing to understand is that your full cooperation is required at all times. When a phase of practice is finished, you must know everything that the coach intended you to learn in that portion of time. Don't be hesitant about asking questions if you are not sure that you understood what was covered. For example, if a coach were explaining what the coverage would

be versus a twin right formation when a man went in motion, you must understand what you are required to know and do. If you never understood it in practice, it could cost the team a touchdown in the next game.

Obviously, there can be no clowning or fooling around at practice. The coach has put a great deal of time into trying to get the players blended into a team, and each and every practice brings you one day closer to being a good team. Players who don't pay attention or who fail to do what they are asked to do can completely disrupt a practice and will hurt the team.

USE OF DRILLS TO IMPROVE SKILLS

Many individual drills were offered earlier in this text as they related to certain positions. They are only a few of the specialized drills that exist. In fact, a book could be written on just the wide variety of drills that different teams use in their attempt to make their players as good as they can be.

Other drills have a more general value; that is, they apply to all football players, not just selected positions. These come under the heading

CARIOCA DRILL

RUNNING BACKWARD DRILL

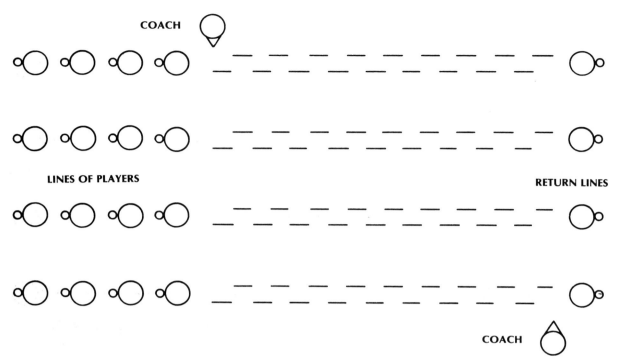

of conditioning, agility, and reaction drills. They involve a whole assortment of activities and are usually done during the team's preseason period, when the coaching staff is conducting practice sessions. Thereafter, some of them continue to be used every day during the season's practice periods because of their great value to the players. The most popular of these are illustrated in the diagram on page 151.

Agility drills are important to every member of the team. Perhaps the best of them is the carioca drill, because it requires the players to develop a full control of their bodies, arms, legs, and feet. With about four rows of players, all facing one sideline, they must turn the palms of their hands skyward as their arms are extended to their sides to their fullest. The first boys in each row must then begin to run sideward with their left legs crossing over their right legs as they develop a rhythm of stride to carry them all the way down the field. The second boys in each row start in the same fashion as soon as the first wave has gone five yards, and so on. When they all get to the far end of the field, they regroup and start again in exactly the same format. Any boy doing this for the first time will find it very

difficult and awkward but, after doing it often enough, the entire team will become as graceful as ballerinas on a stage. The improvement will mean that their agility has improved (see diagram above).

The running backward drill is organized in much the same way. Begin with the same number of lines, evenly spaced apart as is necessary in all drills, and have them turn their backs to the far goal line. On the call of "go," the first wave begins to run backward down the field. Running backward is a skill that can be developed with practice. It requires the raising of the legs after a good push-off from the feet as though you were shoving yourself off a diving board on a back flip. It also requires a well-timed pumping motion of the arms to keep the legs in rhythm. Without this rhythm, the boys will trip and fall over backward. This is the same pumping motion of the arms that is so vital to increasing the forward running speed (see diagram on page 153).

The run and turn drill is another that concentrates on the leg and foot movement of the player. From the same lines arrangement, the players start from their position's stance and run

RUN AND TURN DRILL

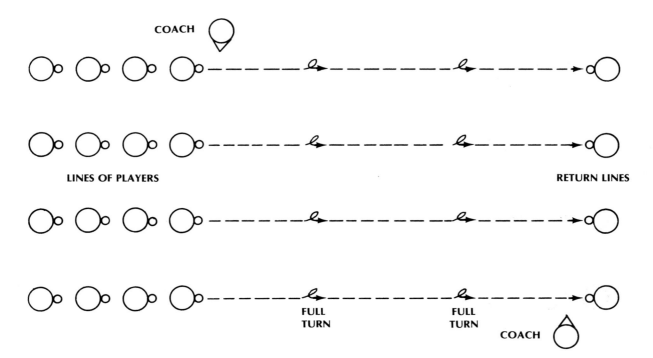

at half speed for ten yards after the first whistle from the coach. On the second whistle they make a full turn, going completely around, and continue running for another ten yards. Then a third whistle signifies that they must make another full turn and then open up to sprint the last ten yards with all the speed they can muster. The importance of this drill is to develop the ability to keep the body under full control as the feet and legs turn the body around without tripping or falling. This is very hard to do at first but will get easier as the season progresses (see diagram at top of page 154).

The drum major drill is begun from the same lineup and calls for each player to run at a rather slow pace, almost at half speed. The emphasis on this drill is the exaggeration of the running technique, as seen when a drum major rushes out onto the field to lead the band during the halftime ceremonies at a college football game. Each player should arch his back, holding his head back and his chin up, as he pumps his knees almost up to his chest and as his arms extend from his waist up into the air above his head. Each step should only be about a half yard long and the players should stress timing and

rhythm rather than speed. It is a coordination and conditioning drill as well as an agility drill and will give the player better control over the movements of his body (see diagram at bottom of page 154).

The gestapo drill is called that because it looks like the marching style of the German Army in World War II. The upper body activities are the same as in the drum major drill above, but the legs and feet are much different. Now we are looking for the longest stride possible with the weight landing on the heels and not the toes as in normal running. Further, no attempt should be made to bend the knees. Rather, the legs should come up stiffly from the hip and the heels should be dug into the turf when they hit the ground. The real value of this drill is to make the boys bounce and spring off the ground and to get full coordination of their arms and legs. Because it is an unnatural way to run, it forces the boys to control their every movement, which is what coordination and agility are all about.

Another excellent drill is the mirror drill. This is done best by pairing up boys who play the same positions. Allow enough room between

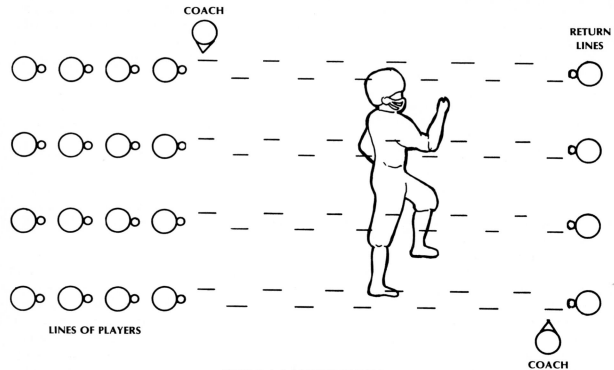

DRUM MAJOR DRILL

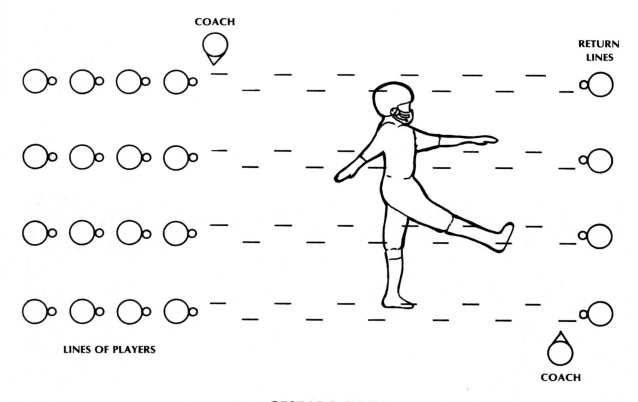

GESTAPO DRILL

pairs because they require a good deal of area to perform the drill. At the start, one boy of each pair is designated as the leader and the other is the follower. The leader then begins to do a wide variety of movements and the follower must do the same thing as quickly as he can. The leader may, for example, drop to his stomach flat on the ground, get up quickly and run in place with his knees pumping up to his chest as in the drum major drill, turn quickly by jumping and turning 90 degrees to his left, then turn 180 degrees to his right; then drop to a pushup position and do five quick pushups; then roll over on his back and do five leg lifts; then do a few somersaults.

After the leader has had his turn, the follower becomes the leader and he puts his partner through an even tougher pace. It is a fun drill but also develops reaction capability and the boys learn to be quick and to control their movements.

As stated earlier, these are but a few of the drills that many coaches use. By doing them all well, you will improve significantly in your body control and coordination.

CALISTHENICS AND ENDURANCE TRAINING

This portion of practice is usually liked the least by football players because it not only represents a good deal of work, but it also includes no playing with the ball. As is true of many other aspects of the game, this phase has changed, too. Many years ago calisthenics meant pushups, jumping jacks, running in place, leg raises, and so on. It was known as the exercise period because it was just like what went on in the physical education period during school.

As football made the switch to greater emphasis on body building through extensive weights programs, it was no longer necessary to spend team practice time doing the old body-building things. Rather, it became a time to limber up and stretch the muscles that perhaps were becoming tight and taut from their weight-lifting activities. Calisthenics soon became a series of stretching actions, all designed to warm up and loosen up the players' bodies before practice and before games.

Most practice sessions begin with some form of running, either the running drills described earlier in this chapter or simply a few laps around the field. This is considered a warm-up activity. The really hard running in the form of fast wind sprints is saved for the end of practice because it takes so much out of everyone. Doing it in the beginning would make the players very weary for the entire session.

After the initial warm-up running, the technique now being used is handled as shown in the diagram on page 156. The players are asked to form a series of concentric circles with the captains in the center. Facing the center, everyone begins a long series of stretching activities. The first one is a leg stretching exercise in which one leg is extended as far forward as possible, knee bent, and all the body weight is leaned forward on it. Both hands are used to press

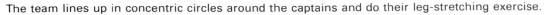

The team lines up in concentric circles around the captains and do their leg-stretching exercise.

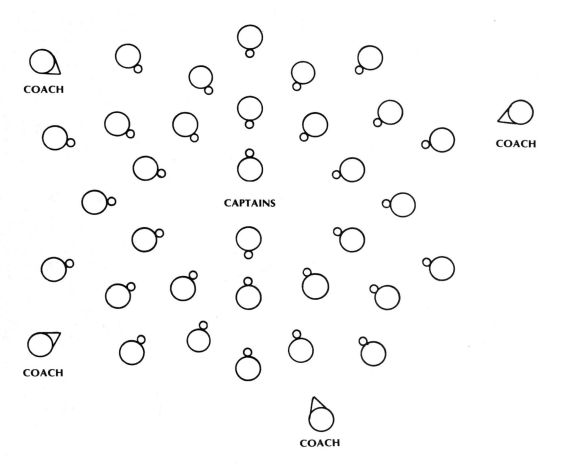

COACH

COACH

CAPTAINS

COACH

COACH

STRETCHING FORMATION

down on the front thigh just above the knee. While this is being done, the rear leg, which is stretched out to its limit in the opposite direction, must also have downward pressure applied on it to contract its muscles. After being held in this position for about one minute, the legs are reversed and a minute is spent doing the same thing to the other leg. During these stretches, the groin area is getting some benefits because all of its muscles and ligaments are feeling the pressure as well.

The next action is a standing toe pull exercise. The players place their feet about six inches apart, bend over at the waist without any knee bend at all, and place the fingers of each hand under the toes of the shoe. Once placed, the hands pull up on the toes and tug until they feel the pressure on the entire backs of their legs,

from the Achilles tendon behind the ankles up to its other end at the top of their legs. This position is held for another minute, after which the players straighten up to give their back muscles a thirty-second break from the stress of this exercise.

The third act, the crossed feet stretch, is very similar to the second. The players now cross their feet so tightly together that the sides of their shoes actually touch. The left foot is where the right one usually is and the reverse is true for the right one. Once again, with no bend of the knees, the players lean over as far as they can, first to touch the turf in front of their toes and later to get their palms to touch flat on the turf. This really stretches out the leg muscles and gets them fully ready for running at full speed. It has been found that this exercise has

The players lean over without bending their knees and put their fingers under the fronts of their shoes and pull up on their toes to stretch out their leg muscles.

reduced the incidence of muscle pulls so common in athletes who run at wide-open speeds in their sport. After a minute with the feet in this

The players turn on one side and extend one leg out and pull the other leg back in the same position as a track hurdler going over a hurdle.

alignment, they are reversed and the entire action is repeated with the new positioning of the feet.

The fourth drill, called the hurdle drill, is done while the players are sitting on the surface with one leg (left) turned on its side with the foot pointing at twelve o'clock and the other (right), also on its side, pointing to four o'clock in a hurdling position. The player now grabs the laces with his right hand and pulls the heel of the right shoe back against his right rump. While the heel is touching, he pulls the toes back and tries to point them at six o'clock. All of this backward pressure will force the player to lean far back on his left elbow until his back is practically on the ground. The extensive stretching of the knee, thigh muscles, hip, ankle, and foot caused by this drill makes it almost a complete body stretch. After a minute, the legs are reversed and the entire drill is repeated from the other side.

After they sit up at the end of this exercise to begin the sitting toe pull, they sit erect with their feet extending straight ahead, parallel with each other, with the inside ankles held firmly together. With legs flat on the ground, they lean

With everyone sitting on the ground, the players reach out and pull back on their toes to stretch their backs.

forward and once again grab the tips of their shoes and pull back with all their strength. This is another leg stretch, but it also puts great pressure on the back muscles as the body tries to pull the hands off their hold on the feet.

When this is held for a minute, while the players are still sitting they grab both ankles and pull the heels of both feet up tight to their buttocks for the squeeze drill. This presses the knees firmly against the chest and completes the stretching of the muscles around the hips and lower back, with the leg muscles completely contracted against each other.

This concludes the six different stretching exercises. With all the pulling pressure involved, the muscles of the arms, neck, and shoulders have been warmed up while those of the back, hips, legs, and feet have also been put through a good workout, which is what this is all about. Doing these drills faithfully every day in conjunction with weight training and running drills is all a player needs to get himself ready to play the game of football.

The requirement for endurance is best satisfied through the running program, which builds strength and in turn creates the stamina that every player must have to sustain him throughout the game and the season. In addition, the strength development of the body gives it a greater tolerance for the rigors of the season and makes it possible for a player to perform at a higher level than ever before.

While sitting, the players pull the heels of their feet up tight against their butts to stretch the hip and back.

18 | The Special Skills of Punting and Kicking

Many coaches have come to realize the importance of the kicking game in football. In this connection, the term *kicking* means both punting the ball and place-kicking it. Perhaps the growth in popularity of the professional game has underscored the importance of place-kicking in the offensive scoring department, but the efficiency of the total kicking game is thoroughly recognized as a requirement for success. Any young player would do well to attempt to get involved in this area, at least to the extent that he should try his hand at it. It may be surprising to see that, with a little instruction and a great deal of practice, you can become good at it.

PUNTING TECHNIQUES

You must learn to do a number of things in order to punt consistently well. To be consistent

means to punt spirals most of the time, say, seven out of every ten. Let's identify each thing you must learn and discuss how and why each must be done.

The first is the stance. When you, as a punter, are waiting for the snap from the center, you should have your kicking leg about six inches behind your front foot. When the ball is in the air en route to you, step forward on the front foot to catch it. This becomes the first step of your three-step approach to punting the ball.

Your body should be leaning forward at the waist, your eyes focused intently on the ball in much the same fashion as a wide receiver who is getting ready to receive a pass. If you should drop the snap from center, if will often mean a fumble recovery or a blocked punt for the opposition. It would be a vital mistake and the team would suffer greatly.

As you begin taking your steps to deliver the

The punter moves forward as he comes off his second step and drops the ball while bringing his kicking leg to it.

punt, you must begin moving the ball around in your hands to get the laces almost to the outside edge of the ball to avoid having them touch your shoe when you make contact with it. At the same time, you should grasp the lower front part of the ball with your left hand (assuming you are a right-footed kicker) while your other hand holds the lower right quarter of the ball, with its palm facing up. Once you have full control of the ball, you should pull in your arms with the elbows held snugly to the body.

As it rests in your hands, the ball should be turned slightly toward the left and never straight ahead toward the goal line. If you were in midfield, directly in line between the goalposts, the ball would be pointed at a spot midway between the goalposts and the corner of the end zone. The steps forward should be short, something less than your normal stride.

The length of the steps differs with each player because it is influenced by the height of the punter and the length of his legs. As you come off your second step, your arms should extend the ball gently forward as though you were making an offering of a loaf of bread to a customer in a restaurant. The hands should then begin to lower the ball to its final drop position.

The drop distance should be as short as you

can make it and still maintain your balance and rhythm. If the ball is dropped too far, it will have a greater chance to turn and may change the angle of the ball when it hits the foot. If it is dropped properly, the ball will be pointing slightly downward at the front, which will expose its rear underpart to the same angle that the foot has when it comes off the ground heading for its impact on the ball. If the surface of the foot meets squarely with the surface of the ball, maximum contact will be made.

Contact on the foot should be made on the area to the side of the shoe's laces, under which is the main and strongest bone in the foot. The ball is not kicked with the toes; in fact, the toes should be bent downward in order to raise the strong bone in the middle of the foot under the laces. It is the intent of the punter to make a strong impact on the ball with this bone in order to give the ball its strongest blow.

The leg and foot should travel on an arc that comes up from the outside of the foot toward the direction in which the nose of the ball was pointed. This crossing impact under the rear of the ball gives it the spin that creates the spiral, and it is the spiral that allows the ball to travel efficiently through the air. The spiral does not incur any additional wind drag; thus, it travels farther than a ball that doesn't spiral. When the ball starts upward as a spiral and turns over and

As the ball points slightly down and in, the punter turns his toes down and swings his foot upward toward the middle, underpart of the ball.

After contact, the punter's kicking leg is fully extended forward, toes bent downward, arms out wide, and the bottom foot well off the ground.

spirals downward, too, then it has been kicked perfectly. If you fail to make the ball spiral, you have to adjust the way you hold the ball, drop it, and the cross-cutting of it when your foot makes contact. This assumes that you are making contact with the proper area of your foot.

The last phase of the punt is the follow-through. After you have punted the ball, your toes should be pointing downward, your kicking leg should be extended fully into the air, your arms should be fully extended outward toward your sides to maintain your balance, and your back (or bottom) foot should be well off the ground. This last thing is very important because if you are not fully off the ground, it means that you have not come up through the ball with enough force to get yourself off the ground. This, in turn, means that you have not punted the ball as hard as you can. Work on it because it can make the difference between an average punter and a good one.

Practice and Training to Improve

Learning to punt well is a matter of constant practice after you have developed the proper form for your body. You should try to punt at least twenty times every day, but any more than

that may make your leg tired and cause you to alter your delivery slightly, which could get you into some bad habits. Be sure to have your coach observe your technique if you are not improving your delivery. Sometimes it is easy for someone else to see what you can't see that may be causing you trouble.

Many punters are finding that by building up the strength of their legs they are able to increase their distance. This is not surprising because, to some degree, punting is a matter of the speed at which you can propel your leg in an upward arc. The faster the leg comes off the ground, the more velocity it will have when it makes contact with the ball. However, consistently good punting depends more on the timing and rhythm of the approach to the point of contact and the follow-through after contact. You will never see a good punter with a jerky movement in his delivery. Rather, you will see a smooth, gliding motion from the moment he catches the ball until he comes down to the ground after his follow-through.

It is not uncommon for players who want to be their team's punter to practice year-round. The muscles you use for this action are unique to football. If you stop punting during the year, these muscles will lose their tone and you will have to go back to the beginning when you start again later in the year. This is one skill that you can improve entirely by yourself. Get a couple of balls, go out into a field, and punt to your heart's content. Then run downfield to build up your legs and punt the balls back down again. It's up to you to decide how much you want to train.

Kicking Techniques

There are two different ways of place-kicking the football. The oldest style is often called the traditional way because it goes back to the beginning of football. This is the straight-on approach in which the ball is kicked by a square-toed shoe off the front of the foot. The other is the soccer style of kicking, often referred to as the sidewinding way of kicking, kicked off the side of the foot.

There is some degree of controversy as to which is the better way. Some coaches, and they may tend to be the older coaches, feel that the straight-on approach is best because it gets the ball up in the air higher and sooner in a shorter distance, thus avoiding blocked kicks. Proponents also believe that the straight-on style is more accurate because the ball is not likely to hook as much as the soccer style kicker's ball hooks.

On the other side of the argument, the supporters of the soccer approach feel that the ball can be kicked farther because the whole side of the foot becomes the kicking surface, rather than just the front surface. They also believe distance can be increased because the arc of the kicking foot travels farther and therefore gives the soccer kicker greater velocity when he makes contact with the ball.

As far as young players are concerned, the technique that you learn should be based once again on your body structure rather than on someone's opinion about which provides the better results. If you are heavy-legged and have powerful thigh and calf muscles, the traditional method will probably give you the best chance of success. On the other hand, if your legs are more slender and have long, rather than chunky, compact muscles, then the soccer style may be the best way for you to go. These are general guidelines and they should not be considered rigid. If you want to be a kicker, you should try both ways and determine for yourself which way you would prefer to kick.

The straight-on style requires you to choose one of two basic ways of kicking. One requires only one step to be taken and the other is a two-step approach. In the one-step, assuming you are a right-footed kicker, you start with your kicking foot about a shoe's length ahead of your back foot. You must lean forward at the hip with both arms hanging and your eyes fixed firmly on the kicking toe. When you placed the tee on the ground you made sure that it was pointing directly at the center of the goalposts as though you were setting your sights on it for the accuracy of your kick.

The distance you should stand from the tee should be the length of a long, leaping stride, which would bring the front of your left foot to a point even with the back of the tee. As you are looking forward for the arrival of the ball into the holder's hands, you must shift your weight with a short jab step onto your right foot, take a

The kicker leans forward at the hip, both arms hanging, and takes a long, leaping stride away from the tee.

long, leaping step with your left foot, and swing your kicking leg into the ball. While you are doing this, the holder is receiving the ball, turning it to get the laces to face the goalposts, and placing it down on the kicking tee in a straight up-and-down position. It must not be tilted in any direction. A tilt to the left or the right, as the kicker looks at the ball, will make it go either to the left or to the right of the goalposts.

At the moment of impact, you must have your ankle and knee in a locked position, much as though you had only one bone in your entire leg. The leg must swing on an axis from its hip in order to give it the most velocity. The toes on the kicking foot should be bent upward to add rigidity to the foot and to lock the shoe firmly on the foot. The point of impact on the ball should be just slightly below its midpoint. This will permit the longest distance that can be achieved.

Once again, the follow-through is of utmost importance. This is the action that gives the ball

The holder reaches forward for the ball with one knee on the ground and the other leg pointing at the center.

The holder puts the ball down on the tee, straight up and down, with no lean in any way and laces to the front.

At impact, the kicker's ankle and knee are locked, with his kicking leg swinging from the hip as he tries to raise his toe up into the sky with a powerful thrust.

its elevation and, whether you're kicking extra points, field goals, or kickoffs, high kicks are an advantage. In the first two cases, it makes blocking them more difficult. In the last case, high kickoffs give the kicking team more time to get downfield to tackle the ball carrier before he is able to come too far upfield. It is all in the follow-through and leg lift.

After the ball is kicked, you must keep your head down with your eyes still fixed on the ground. This avoids any loss of follow-through that could be caused by raising your head to see where the ball went. From the moment you stand ready for the snap to the moment that you make your follow-through, you must picture the goalposts in your mind, and you must try to

After impact, the kicker keeps his head down to avoid any loss of follow-through caused by raising the head.

raise your leg upward, directly at the center of the goalposts as though you were steering the ball in that direction.

In the two-step approach, the kicker must move another half step farther back from the tee. Instead of taking a short jab step as you did in the one-step, you take a full stride with the kicking leg, take the long leaping step with the other leg, and kick the ball. This technique is used by players who can't achieve as much distance with the one-step because it provides more momentum going into the ball. Sometimes, one-step kickers switch to the two-step when they have a long field goal to attempt.

Regardless of which technique is used—whether the kicker uses the two-inch tee to get the ball up higher or the one-inch tee, which tends to provide more distance—the tee should be placed about seven yards off the line of scrimmage. This has been determined to be the safest place in the backfield to avoid having the kick blocked. When the tee is closer to the line of scrimmage, the interior defensemen have a better chance to get their arms on the ball because the ball will not have a chance to get up high enough. When it is farther away from the line of scrimmage, the outside defenders have a better chance to get in and dive at a spot in front of the kicker to block the kick. The seven-yard distance forces them to rush around the outside

blocker and to turn in, which causes them to lose some speed.

The soccer-style kicker makes contact with the ball on the instep of his foot to the left of the laces. He is using the weight of the entire foot but is trying to make contact with the same big bone under the laces that the punter uses to get maximum force into the ball. As opposed to the direct approach to the ball that the straight-on kicker uses, the soccer-style kicker comes at the ball from a 45-degree angle. All of them use a two-step approach, but the length of the steps vary, depending on the length of the kicker's legs and his need for more or less velocity getting into the ball.

After the tee is placed and pointed at the goalposts, you stand a few yards back, lining up the tee with the goalposts like a gun sight. You then take two short steps to the left (assuming you are a right-footed kicker) and stand with your left foot pointing at the tee; the right foot is about eighteen inches farther back, with its toe pointing at the sideline. Most of your weight should be on the front foot and your body should be leaning toward the goalposts. Although your eyes must be on the kicking tee, you must pick up the flight of the ball as it starts on its way back from the center. The sighting of the ball is your trigger to begin your approach to the tee.

One soccer-style kicker is poised in his starting stance while the other has already taken his first step.

The soccer-style kicker's follow-through carries his kicking leg on a long, sweeping arc as his body turns around.

The first step is taken with your back foot. It should be a crossing step to cover a little less than half the distance between your stance and the ball. The original distance from the ball varies with the stride of the kicker but is usually about three yards for high school and college players, less for younger players. After the first step is taken, you must push strongly off that foot to launch your body toward the tee.

The last step is a leaping one. You land with the left foot about eight to ten inches to the side of the ball, trying to land with your left heel parallel to the tee and pointing toward the goalposts. At the point of contact just below the midpoint of the ball, your body is leaning backward away from the kicking foot as you balance yourself for the long sweeping arc of the kicking leg.

The follow-through results in the kicking leg swinging around all the way to your left, actually turning your body around from the force of its sweeping motion. The arc must be an upward swing to get the ball airborne as soon as possible and to give it the height it needs to carry for a long distance.

There are two basic problems with this style of kicking. As stated earlier, the ball has a tendency to hook from right to left. This can

happen when the holder allows the ball to tilt to the left, in which case it is not the kicker's fault. However, if the kicker's arc is allowed to sweep too far from sideline to sideline, rather than from bottom to top, the ball will hook rather than go straight. The same effect is seen when the foot makes contact too far forward of the big bone under the laces. The opposite effect, pushing the ball to the right of the goalposts, occurs when the foot makes contact too far to the rear of the foot. This does not permit the ball to hook at all, and the kicker, who learns to allow for the hook, particularly on long field goals, gets no hook at all and misses to the right.

PRACTICE AND TRAINING TO IMPROVE

Kicking is similar to punting in terms of practice and training. You must get your technique down to the best actions to suit your build and coordination, and then you must get as much practice as you can to repeat and repeat the style you feel is best for you. The punter has it a little better than you because he can practice by himself. You can do many things by yourself but, to get the most out of extra point and field goal practice, you need a center and a holder to include the timing of the snap and the placement of the ball on the tee. However, you can use the kickoff tee as a holder to give your leg and body the workout they need to keep your kicking performance at the level you want to maintain.

The use of the kickoff tee is vital to your kickoff practice. The only variation between the other place kicks and the kickoff is the distance behind the ball from which you start. This also varies considerably from one kicker to another. For the straight-on kicker, the distance should be anywhere from five to nine yards back. A good technique is to measure your steps backing away from the ball, actually counting out the steps it takes to reach your starting point. If you find that you get good results, take those measured steps every time and get accustomed to the timing that is involved.

Your approach to the ball should be an ever-accelerating movement, with the first few steps taken at half speed and the speed stepped up as you near the ball. Your objective should be to

The straight-on kicker's foot must contact the ball just below the midpoint to allow it to turn slowly in the air.

The soccer-style approach is taken from a 45-degree angle as he whips his leg into a powerful arc into the ball.

move briskly into the ball at the time of contact so that your momentum can add to the velocity of the kick. You must also be certain that your last step places your nonkicking foot at a point a few inches behind the ball.

The best way to judge this is to evaluate the spin of the ball on its flight downfield. If it is spinning too quickly, your front foot was too far forward when your kicking foot made contact with the ball. If the ball is barely rotating, or turning slowly, your kick is perfect and you should try to put your front foot at the same distance from the ball every time you kick. As is true of the field goal, the best place to contact the ball is just below the midpoint. When you hit this spot the ball not only spins more slowly, it also travels farther for the same reason the spiral goes farther on a punt. Less wind drag affects it. If you kick too high on the back of the ball, it will either float or wobble, often not getting high off the ground. The follow-through on the kickoff makes the difference between a long kick and an average one. A good follow-through includes a strong leg lifting motion that not only generates more distance, but also gets more elevation to allow the kickoff team to get downfield to cover the return.

The soccer-style approach to the ball on a kickoff is done from the same angle that the field goal was approached. Some soccer-style kickers start from only four yards away from the ball while some start from five to ten yards away. Your own preference must be determined after practicing at various distances. All the same techniques used for the field goal are used for the kickoff, but the velocity of the kick is considerably greater because of the distance of the approach.

The placement of the ball on the tee for either style of kicking is practically the same. If you want greater distance because you are getting all the height you want, the ball should be placed straight up on the tee, perpendicular to the playing field. This exposes the "sweet spot" (the best place to kick the ball) to contact by the kicker's foot. On the other hand, if you are not getting enough height, the ball should be leaned or tilted slightly backward toward your goal line. This gives it a better elevation angle and will allow the ball to go higher. However, it reduces the frequency with which you will hit the sweet spot because it will be turned slightly under the back side of the ball. This in turn may reduce your distance. Experiment and, through constant practice, you will find the best angle for your style.

Remember that the best way to improve your kicking is to kick often and to have your legs in the best possible shape. All the leg strengthening activities covered in earlier chapters will help.

19 | Kickoff and Punting Teams— Offensive and Defensive

SELECTION OF FORMATIONS AND THEIR PERSONNEL—KICKOFFS AND PUNTS

This chapter will cover the responsibilities of the special team players on kickoffs and punts, both the kicking teams and the receiving teams. Much has been said for years about the importance of the special teams and, for this reason, coaches are very anxious to have their teams prepared to handle both sides of the kicking game. They will also put in many hours of practice time throughout the season to constantly try to improve the performances of the players.

For years no changes were made in the kickoff formation. Eleven players were lined up across the field and the middle guy, the kicker, simply strode forward and kicked the ball. In the never-ending attempt to improve the offensive side of the kickoff, coaches designed special return

plays and many kickoffs were run back for touchdowns. To counter the increase in long returns, kickoff formations and strategy began to change. Now a variety of different formations is used, and kickers try to kick the ball in different ways to avoid returns.

One of the new kickoff formations is shown in the diagram on page 168. The basic formation is not too different from kickoff formations of the past. However, one player on each side is like a wild card on his side of the field. These two players may decide to rush downfield between any of the players on their side. The purpose of this technique is to prevent the receiving team from knowing the location of all eleven men coming down the field to make the tackle on the ball carrier.

These wild card players may also be specifically directed by the special team's coach to run into a certain slot and head for a given spot on

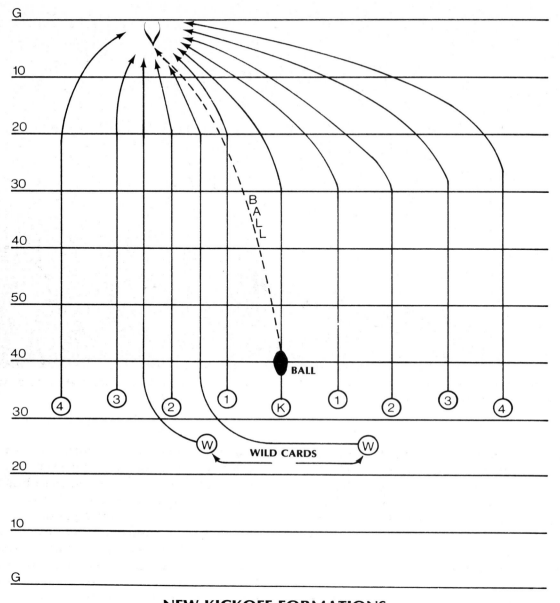

NEW KICKOFF FORMATIONS

the field. Let's take the situation in which the receiving team has an outstanding return specialist, who lines up on their left hash mark near the five-yard line. The kicking team does not want him to get the ball because they are afraid that he might break one for a touchdown.

The coach gives the kicker instructions to kick the ball into the opposite corner of the field to force the other deep returner to handle the ball. And, because the ball is going there, he tells the two wild cards to circle around behind the other

four players on the left side and sprint down toward the receiving team's right corner.

Another special situation is the execution of an on-side kick. Once again, the coach may direct the two wild cards to head for the side of the field toward which the kicker is going to squib the ball. Because of their speed, they might recover the ball. The other members of the kickoff team have specific jobs to do and areas to cover. Let's look at them, one by one.

The two 4 men are usually fast defensive

The socker-style kicker kicks off to his deep left as the two wild card members of the team race down the left side to get the ball carrier inside the twenty.

backs. Their role is to streak downfield as fast as they can and to ensure that no return comes around their end. When they see the ball going elsewhere, they must take their angle of pursuit to get in on the tackle, but they must always make sure that the ball is not coming back to their side on a reverse.

The 3 men are often fast defensive ends or linebackers. They must be good tacklers and strong enough to break through hard blocks to make the tackle. Because they are closer to the middle of the field, they will see plenty of action as they pursue the ball carrier. They must be careful not to converge in toward the middle too soon or they will leave their lanes unprotected. These lanes are important to make sure that the entire width of the field has a defender in place to make a tackle.

The 2 men usually are backup running backs or tight ends. The coach wants people who are fast, with enough body weight to avoid being knocked over easily. Their lanes are closer to the middle of the field, which places them in the

area where they will encounter the wall of a center return if the receiving team uses that return play. Their quickness will also help them avoid blockers and get to the ball carrier.

The players who get the 1 positions are usually the biggest, fastest players, who often are not first-stringers on either offense or defense. They must break up the blocking in the middle by bursting through the wedge blockers on the middle return. And, if they can't make the tackle, they must take down as many of the blockers in front of the ball carrier as they can.

The wild cards head directly for the ball, wherever it goes. Their running start gives them a little more speed than their teammates when the ball is kicked and they must try to avoid downfield blocks in their race to the ball carrier.

All members of the team have to adjust their downfield courses, based on the movement of the ball as it is run upfield, but they must be sure to keep their distances from their teammates or gaping holes may be created in their attack line running down under the kick. Returners are taught to look for daylight in the kicking team and will run through the seams that may be created. The kicker, who is usually not an active defensive player in upper levels, is often an excellent player in lower classes. Based on his coach's wishes, he may either be the middle man running down the field or he may stop after the kick to play the role of middle safety in case a returner makes it past his teammates.

There are other variations of the kickoff team. Some coaches ask their 4 men to go directly for the ball and have their 3 men circle behind them to guard the outside of the field. This is intended to confuse the return team's blocking assignments. Similar tactics may be used for the 1 and 2 men, based on the logic that crossing lanes forces the return team to look for their men and thereby get mixed up.

PUNTING TEAM

The punting team formations are numerous. Two of the more popular ones were reviewed in chapter 10 in our coverage of the use of line splits for offensive blocking (see diagram below). Another favorite of many coaches is shown in the diagram.

This formation uses the principle that, if you put nine players on the line of scrimmage, you are getting them as close to the punt return team as you can. That is one of the two objectives of a punting team—to get downfield and stop the return. The other is to give the punter time to get the punt off without allowing it to be blocked.

This formation calls for line splits of one yard between each of the players, which spreads them

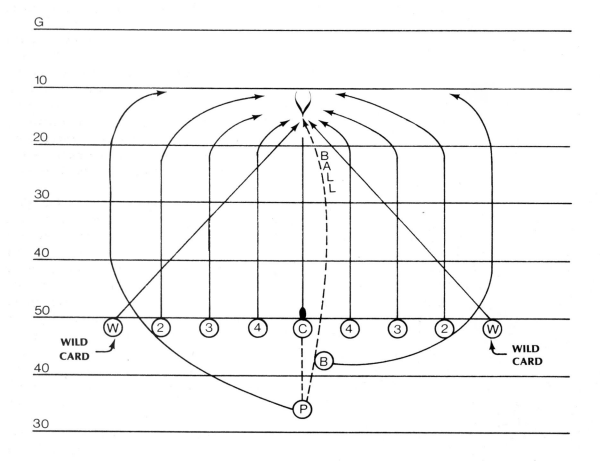

PUNT FORMATION

out across a good portion of the field. This is an important aspect of preventing the return team from running the ball back around their left or right side. The same coverage that is necessary on a kickoff team that requires the players to keep in lanes applies to the punting team, too. Starting from a spread formation helps keep the lanes apart. And, if the punt goes to the left or right, the men going downfield have to adjust their lanes to head for the ball. The outside men on the line of scrimmage are the same kinds of defensive backs that play the wild cards on the kickoff team. They must bump anyone on their inside gap and speed down the field to wherever the ball goes. Because of their speed and outside location, they are expected to be the first men at the ball and should make most of the tackles.

The second men in are often either the backup running backs from the kickoff team or are fast linebackers who can cover the outside when they loop outside the defensive backs. Their blocking assignments are the same as every other player on the line of scrimmage in to the center. The blocking rule is a matter of priorities. The first is to block anyone on their inside gap. If no one is there, they must block anyone on their head. If no one is there, they must block the outside gap. Finally, if no one is there, they block the most dangerous man close to them. The block consists only of a solid shoulder block to break

The center tilts the ball upward as both hands are poised ready to pull it and spin it to the kicker.

the stride of the defender to prevent him from going in at full speed. After the block, they all release quickly to stop the return.

The third men in from the end are usually fast tight ends who have shown good tackling skills. Their larger stature provides stronger blocking power to cope with the big people that the return team may use in the middle of their line if they are going to try to block the kick. A strong shoulder block is needed by a big lineman to stop hard-charging big linemen from the other team. But their speed is needed to get downfield.

The fourth players in are the big players next to the center. It is their job first to guarantee that no opponent is allowed to go through the slots on either side of the center because that is how most punts are blocked. The coach will often use big defensive ends or any other fast big men who can block and tackle. These are key people in the heart of the punting team and they must do their jobs well.

The center must ensure a good snap or the punting team will be in deep trouble. For some reason, even the upper levels of ball sometimes have difficulty finding a player who can perform this important function well. If the player who wins this job is also big, it will help both the punting team and the field goal/extra point team because the defense will put many people around him to blast up the middle to block a kick or punt.

The proper technique for snapping for punts and kicks requires the center to hold the ball with his left hand on the top, forward, left part of the ball, nearer the middle of the ball rather than the point. His right hand should be under the bottom, right, forward part of the ball, nearer the point than the middle. By pulling the ball back toward the punter through his legs, the center must spin his hands in a clockwise direction to get the ball to spiral in its flight. The use of his fingers is important to making the ball spiral because their placement on the ball can make the difference between success and failure.

Equally important to the quality of the snap is the placement of the center's legs when he takes his stance. His body weight must be balanced to allow only a slight pressure on the ball at the moment the snap is started. This requires him to get his legs a few inches wider than his shoulders and to lean forward just a bit as he lowers into his squat position. When he raises the ball at the start of the snap, he practically throws it between his legs into the backfield.

Snaps to punters should be aimed to their kicking leg's side to enable them to catch the ball as they stride forward to begin the punt delivery. Snaps for place kicks should be directed at the holder's hands, wherever the coach wants them held. Only with constant practice can the snap to both of these players become a routine action. But, if you can learn to do it well, you have an excellent chance of winning the job on your team.

HOW TO BLOCK THE PUNT OR PLACE KICK

The most accepted way of blocking punts and place kicks is to attack a specific area on the line of scrimmage with deception and strength. A commonly used technique is shown in the diagram above. Both men on the line of scrimmage must be strong and quick to rush across the heads of the blockers and force them to block the rush at their kicker. If the rushers do their job effectively, a hole or gap should be opened up to

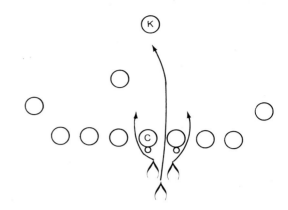

KICK-PUNT BLOCK STUNT

allow the linebacker to power himself into the backfield and block the kick.

The same arrangement can be set up in other areas on the line of scrimmage if you are certain that the ball is going to be kicked. The reason for this is that it takes three players to execute this attack and it does not permit adequate coverage in other areas of concern for the punt-receiving team.

If the coach wants to send the entire receiving team into the punting or kicking backfield for an all-out rush at the kicker, then the kick-blocking plan seen in the diagram could be

An attempt to block the place kick up the middle or through the end fails as the ball flies clear.

KICK-PUNT-ALL-OUT RUSH-BLOCK STUNT

used. As the diagram above indicates, ten of the eleven players have an assignment to attempt to penetrate the blocking front. Timing and quickness are vital to begin the attack at the precise moment when the ball is snapped. Care must be taken not to be offsides or to run into the kicker. It is certainly worth trying at least once each game.

HOW TO RETURN THE PUNT OR KICKOFF— FORMATIONS AND PERSONNEL

The other end of the kicking game is the return of the kickoff and the punt. Coaches have found that by making sound blocking plans it is often possible to make good runbacks. They also realized that a good runback provides their offensive team with good field position where they could use all their effective weaponry. Many teams are reluctant to use their passing game if they are deep in their end of the field.

Some of the necessities for good returns are common to both. Good blocking must be provided through speed and technique, and a fast running back with good open-field running ability must be available. In addition, all eleven members of the special teams must be alert and aware of what's going on because there are many things that can change as a result of where the ball is kicked.

Kickoff and punt return formations are as numerous as there are players on a team. There are many different wrinkles that each coach may add to help him accomplish what he thinks is the best way to make long runbacks. Therefore, we will only go into one of each and try to

An all-out attempt to block a punt almost succeeds as number 44 dives across in front of the punter.

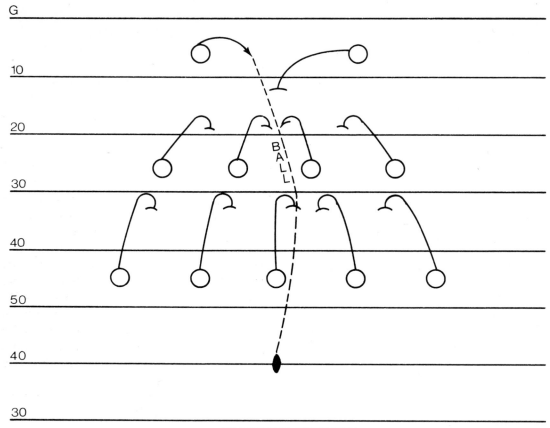

KICKOFF RETURN

describe what the objectives are, many of which can be applied to any formation (see diagram above). This kickoff return provides the basic requirements that each of them must include. First, the front five must be alert for the possibility of an on-side kick. Next, the players in the middle zone between the front five and the deep two must look for a short or squib kick that may bounce along the ground at them. And finally, the deep two should be in an area where the ball may be expected to land so they can catch it in the air and on the run.

The front five have two other concerns. They must avoid having a low kick hit them and bounce off, possibly to their opponents, if they are not careful. And, they must move to the area where the coach wants them to set up and throw their blocks. In this example, they have to run back about fifteen yards. When they arrive, they must turn around, seek out their men, and deliver a crunching shoulder block. Blocks below the waist are not permitted in high school or

college but are allowed in the NFL. The blocks must be intended to knock the defenders off their feet and must be at least strong enough to throw them off balance.

The middle four are asked to move back in relation to the location of the ball, either left or right of center or short or long on the field. Their job is the same as that of the front five as to their blocking instructions: strong shoulder blocks into the area just below the chest. Sometimes determining who to block may be confusing, but the rule is that the outside two look for players coming in from the side and the middle two look for men up the middle. All four must stay no farther apart than within two yards of each other to help ensure that no one comes through the middle of them. They should try to form a moving wall.

The deep two must leave no doubt as to which of them is going to catch the ball. If it is on your side of the center of the field, call out, "I've got it!" The other guy should say, "You've got it" and all confusion should end. The returner should always try to guarantee the catch because a dropped ball on a kickoff may end up as a lost fumble or, at best, poor field position. Don't try to start running until you have caught it. Also, don't catch it while you are backing up if you can avoid it. It's far better to back up a few extra steps while the ball is in flight so you can catch it as you move forward. This enhances your momentum and usually means a few extra yards on the return.

In this return play, the ball is to be run up the middle as the carrier looks for a seam to run through as the blockers upfield do their blocking duties. In order to get as far upfield as possible, the returner must not waste any time on fancy moves until he is near tacklers. Then, sharp movements to the left or right are often the best techniques to slip between defenders to get more yardage. Unless a sideline return play is called, the returner should never run laterally on the field because it will only allow the de-

fenders more time to cover the distance down the field to make the tackle closer to the returner's goal.

The punt return that will be reviewed is shown in the diagram below. In this return, the ball will be returned to the return team's left and will require a number of reactions by its members. The first must be that at least one player goes across the line of scrimmage in an attempt to block the kick. Even if he fails, he will be there if the snap from center is dropped by the punter or if he should try to run or pass the ball. Some amount of attention will be paid to keep the punting team honest. The next requirement is to try to hold up the punting team's players, who will be racing downfield on the snap of the ball. By restraining them as much as possible, the ball returner will have more time to catch the ball and start his run for yardage. The delay tactics must be applied by two quick and strong linebackers who must throw shoulder blocks into their two ends and

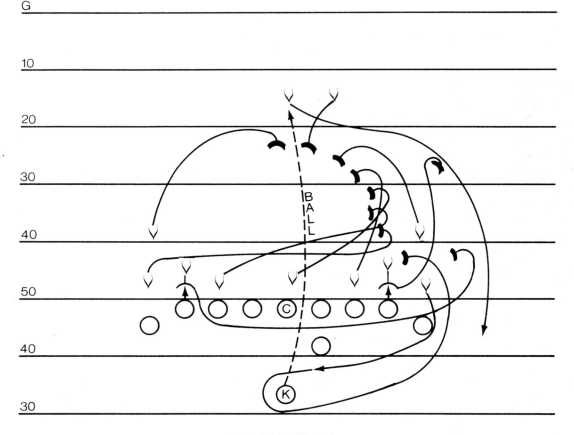

PUNT RETURN

throw them off balance. A second blow may be delivered, if possible.

Next, the return team must protect against a run or pass. These are surprise maneuvers often pulled on an unsuspecting team. To provide the necessary safeguards, the pair of defensive backs who are playing behind the linebackers must read the movements of the punter and, if he doesn't go into his punt delivery, they must look for any receiver coming downfield or into the flat areas. If the punter starts to move into the ball, the defensive backs must retreat toward the twin safeties to get into position for their blocks. They must turn when they are about five yards in front of the returner and look to pick up the men they are going to block. The left defensive back takes the first man on his side of the field and the right defensive back does the same on his side.

While this activity is going on, the other four players on the line of scrimmage are quickly retreating down the field themselves to align themselves in a wall, as diagrammed. The distance they go downfield is also based on the depth of the punt because their blocks will not have too much value if they are thirty yards away from the ball carrier when he streaks up the sideline.

Finally, the twin returner who doesn't catch the ball (after the same exchange of words between them as in the kickoff) must first advise his teammate as to whether he should call a fair catch or not. This is done by looking at how close the opponents will be by the time the ball comes down for the catch. If they will be closer than five yards, he should call, "No," which will tell his teammate to call a fair catch and not attempt a runback. If he says, "Go," it means to catch and run. In addition to this, he must also look to see if the returner has fumbled the ball, in which case two of them will have a better chance of recovery.

The ball carrier must guarantee the catch. That is one of the requirements that the coach looked for when he decided to let this fast, elusive running back or wide receiver start at this position. After the catch, the ball carrier must go directly upfield as fast as he can, making quick changes in direction between defenders if they are there to tackle him. He must try to get behind the wall that his blockers have formed because it will provide a barrier between him and the other defenders who are sprinting downfield to get him. The success of the play depends on how well the wall is formed, how well the blocks are thrown by the members of the wall, and whether the returner can get behind it before he gets tackled. Two very important rules must be remembered: Always hang on to the ball because there are many hard tackles thrown on any return, and never stop to change direction because it gives defenders more time to get close to you. If you must change direction, do it under controlled forward speed, but don't stop. You may not run every punt back for a touchdown, but you should get as much positive yardage as you can. Remember, good field position is the real reason for punt returns.

20 | The Player-Coach Relationship

When a coach undertakes an assignment to coach a football team he makes a commitment to all the players to do all the things that will be required to produce a good team by developing good football players. In order to do this, he will need your help. This chapter will review what he will expect from you to meet his objectives and what you may expect from him to help you become a better player and a better young man.

HONESTY AND STRAIGHTFORWARDNESS

All coaches want their players to be honest young men. This is a necessary quality because it means that the coach will believe you in every situation that develops between you. Honesty begets trust and trust is the ingredient that allows the coach to have faith in you and depend on you.

In his desire to have a winning team, the coach will give you the best technical instructions that he is capable of and he must have faith that you will follow them to the best of your ability. If you prove your honesty by being a straightforward individual, he will see that you are truly trying to perform well and he will be assured of your commitment to the team. On the other hand, if he finds that you have not been honest with him and the team by being unprepared, he will wonder about you every time another situation arises. This will foster a feeling of distrust and may lead him to feel that he cannot depend on you.

Your reputation is the most important thing you own. It must be built on keeping your word and doing the things that you have agreed to do. The coach wants to depend on you as a football player and as a solid young man. Be honest with him by telling him exactly how you feel and he

177

The coach gives the quarter-back directions that he wants carried out as an adjustment to the game plan.

will return your honesty by being fair and straightforward with you.

TEAMWORK

Sometimes a player will get carried away with his own career and fail to recognize that without the other members on the team his performances would be impossible. This can be very disruptive to team unity and coaches try to avoid having it happen on their team. When other players find out that you are more concerned about yourself than about the team, many emotions surface that are not conducive to good teamwork.

Every coach wants every player to put the team ahead of his own desires. For example, you may want to be a running back but the coach feels that the team would be stronger if you played cornerback because you tackle better than anyone else he can put at that position. If your interest is in the team and its potential, you will put your feelings aside and agree to give it your best effort. If you balk at it or sulk about it, the other members of the team will take note of it

and you will lose their respect. It will lead to team discord and that attitude does not promote a winning, cooperative atmosphere.

LOYALTY AND DEPENDABILITY

These are two words heard very often in reference to outstanding members of any team. They imply that a player has done everything he could do for the good of the team because he was loyal to the team and its goals. They also convey that, when it was necessary to get something done, you could depend on a solid effort because of the player's loyalty to the team.

In actual practice a coach looks for dependable athletes who will work hard and do the things he has asked them to do. There are so many things that a football player must do on his own in the way of skills improvements and body building. The coach wants to be able to depend on each player to show his loyalty to the team by getting himself ready for the season. If every player performs all the preseason conditioning requirements, the coach will know that he has a group of boys with whom he can build a winning team.

POSITIVE WINNING ATTITUDE

So much of what football players are able to accomplish is based on their attitude. Attitudes come in two general categories—negative and positive. The negative attitude carries with it a feeling of failure and defeat, but a positive attitude says that, no matter how tough the problem, somehow it can be licked.

Most coaches work very hard to develop a desire for winning. The objectives that are established for each player's ability may mean that he will have to reach out as far as he can to achieve them. But, in reaching for them, he will have to push himself harder than ever before and it is this extreme effort that will show him that he can reach the goal he never dreamed he could reach. Let's take a wide receiver who runs the forty in 4.8 seconds. He dreams of running a 4.5 but doesn't really think he can ever get there. But, by virtue of the positive attitude instilled in him by his coach, he trains and builds his legs up to the point where he finally runs a 4.5 His attitude did it.

A winning attitude includes no taste for losing. When you examine all the requirements for winning and work on them one by one, you will give yourself a much greater chance for success. Your coach will expect you to work on the things that will help the team win. If you're a quarterback, he'll expect you to use your head to figure out which audible to switch to in a tight situation. He will expect the field goal kicker to practice hour after hour to be ready when the team needs a long kick to win the game in the final seconds.

The coach will also expect you never to give up or to quit because you have failed to do something. Turning failure into success is turning from a negative way of thinking to a positive way. Never accept defeat but, rather, set your targets on the contributions you can make to the team and your coach that will bring a victory. You will have to learn to tolerate losing, but you won't have to accept it as a steady diet, not if you have the right attitude.

COOPERATION

When many athletes are involved in a team game like football, all of them must give of themselves for the benefit of the team. A coach will look for you to pull together with him and your teammates to develop a cooperative attitude that will permit the team to be drawn together as a unit. A familiar criticism of a losing team is that they were all looking out for themselves and didn't make the sacrifices that were necessary for the good of the team. This situation often arises when players don't cooperate with the coach and elect to do things their way instead of his way, which is always the team's way.

Cooperation may be reflected in many ways. If the coach asks you to do your school work faithfully, and you do, there will be no problem with your eligibility and the team will benefit by having you on the team. If he asks you to set a good example of what a football player's conduct should be at a dance, then don't let him down by creating a disturbance. If he asks you to run back kickoffs this week because the regular returner is hurt, give him the assurance that you will give it everything you have. If he asks you to take an extra lap around the field because he wants to be sure that you keep your stamina in top condition, do it and don't complain.

A coach doesn't need anyone whose conduct is detrimental to the team, school, or community. Football players are looked up to as symbols of quality young men. You're a reflection on the coach, your classmates, your teammates, and your family. By doing all the things you do every day, on and off the football field, in a way that is admired and respected, you will show your cooperative attitude to everyone associated with you. Your reputation will be everything you could want it to be and you will walk with your head high and be proud of your accomplishments.

WHAT YOU SHOULD EXPECT FROM THE COACH

EVALUATION AND ADVICE

In the normal course of events, the coach will always try to point out to you the areas in which you have to improve. This is necessary for him to do if he is going to get the execution on each play that he wants. Advice of this kind is general advice as he teaches you and the other members

At halftime, the coach reviews with each of his players the things that they will have to do to improve their performances for the remainder of the game.

of the team what to do on offense and defense.

Above and beyond this, however, the coach will always be interested in letting you know how you're doing on an overall basis. You must feel free to question him whenever you feel that a problem may exist to make sure that you understand exactly how he feels about your performance.

A coach is a busy man who has many things to do in the performance of his duty. Although he might like to find the time to talk to each of his players to inform them of his feelings about

their playing ability, he will not always have the time to do it. You should try to approach him when he is not too involved with other things to ask him if there is something you are doing that needs improvement or any other question about your effort that may be on your mind. Feel free to ask him anything; it will be for your benefit and his.

The coach will appreciate your interest and will take the opportunity to clarify things in your mind to make sure you understand. He is just as interested as you are in making certain there is no confusion about technique, execution, or strategy. Don't be hesitant about it. He will think more highly of you for doing it.

INDIVIDUAL ATTENTION

A coach may often find it difficult to get a player to do things his way and, in the busy schedule of events at practice, he may not be able to take the time to review things in sufficient detail for the understanding of each player. If you find that, even though the coach reviewed something in practice, you still don't understand it, ask him to review it with you again.

When there are enough coaches on the staff, it isn't too difficult to get the individual attention that many players require. If you are a running back and have a backfield coach working with you most of the time, he will have time to review anything and everything you may ask for. Don't waste his time unnecessarily, but ask for help when you really need it.

MUTUAL RESPECT AND FAIRNESS

Players usually give their coaches full respect and often treat them as they would their own father. After all, the coach is there because he wants to help you become a good player, and he will give freely of himself to develop your skills and talent. In return for your excellent behavior, he will treat you with mutual respect and will be fair to you in all of his dealings with you. This is almost standard behavior for a coach.

The players who do not act completely above-board will often give the coach many hours of grief in the course of a season. The coach will want to suppress any negative activity that may be occurring because he doesn't want other players to think that he will allow irresponsible behavior. It's sad but true that often just a few boys will disrupt the harmony of a team and force the coach to give them too much of his time.

Players who are intent on having a good season for themselves and for the team realize that they will be treated fairly and with full consideration if they conduct themselves in a wholesome manner. Respect the coach and he will respect you. Try to convince your teammates, who may not be cooperating with the coach, that their approach is bad for them and for the team.

DISCIPLINE

Many people believe that a football team is the last area of our society in which discipline is rigidly enforced. It is a traditional thing that has existed as long as there have been football teams. Some coaches are more intent on it than others, but most believe that a team cannot exist without it.

Discipline really is the establishment of rules and the handing out of punishment if they are broken. Rules are necessary to let all the members of the team know exactly what they are expected to do. They are publicized and talked about often enough to make sure that everyone understands them.

Some of the more important rules govern attendance at practice, curfews for getting home, care of equipment, and getting good grades in school work. Others may involve creating a disturbance at practice, failure to know your assignments on certain plays, and having your playbook up to date and with you at blackboard meetings. The coach cannot afford to have some players do what he wants them to do while others fail to measure up through forgetfulness or carelessness.

As a player, you must learn to live with discipline and understand that it can't be avoided. You will do well to obey all the rules and, if there appears to be a problem that may look as though you are going to break one of them, talk to the coach in advance and let him know what the situation is. For example, if you have to miss a practice for a good reason, have your parents send a note to the coach explaining the problem and let them work out a solution with him.

A coach doesn't always know who he can believe. In order to be sure that his rules and the discipline associated with them are followed, he will often take a hard position with someone if there is no explanation in advance. Don't put him in a spot and make unnecessary trouble for yourself.

An Example of Good Character

Most football coaches believe that a football program is an excellent platform on which to build a solid young man. They will try in every way to direct you and lead you in a way that will make you very proud of yourself. There are many reasons why this is true. Football requires young men to work hard to achieve goals they have set for themselves. As you go through life, you will find one goal after another for which you will strive.

Football also teaches you what is required to be a winner. It forces you to bear up under stress and strain as you cope with one problem after another. Life is filled with problems and, if you don't hold up under the strain, grief will overcome you. Football requires dedication and constant energy to perform the duties of your position. If you carry these qualities forward as you grow older, success will eventually come your way.

The word *character* means that you have good qualities on which you can build a future. It means many other things, too. If you are a dependable team player and make the sacrifices necessary for the good of the team, you have character. If you help an opponent up off the turf after tackling him, you're showing everyone that you are a good sport, and that's character.

If you conduct yourself properly by playing hard, clean football and the opposing coach seeks you out after the game to congratulate you for an excellent game, that's character.

Your coach will give you an example to follow. He will explain why it is necessary to respect yourself, your teammates, and your parents by being honest and dependable in everything you do. You are a representative of your family, your school, and your team, and whatever you do will be a reflection on all of them, not just on yourself. Your coach is responsible for all of his players and he and you must follow the same rules of conduct. It is a commitment you both make when you decide to get involved with a football team. Individuals become members of the team and must shed favorable light on their team.

A Goal for the Future

When youngsters are growing up and getting interested in football, sooner or later they get to see their local high school team play. And, if their love for the game is great enough, they begin to dream of being old enough to be on that team. When they see that the players are proud to be on their team and that they enjoy the friendship and the excitement of competition, the youngsters become even more intent on reaching out for that goal.

Be assured that the goal can be reached and the fun of football can be in your future if you want it badly enough. Give it your best effort and that dream may come true.

Index